The Puppet King

By
Leah Toole

The Puppet King

Copyright © 2023 Leah Toole. All rights reserved.

All rights reserved. No part of this publication may be reproduced, stored, or transmitted in any form or by any means, whether electronic, mechanical, or photocopying, recording, scanning, or otherwise without written permission from the author.
It is illegal to copy this book, post it to a website, or distribute it by any other means without permission.

Praise for the Novels of
The Tudor Heirs Series:

"Been so excited for this to come out after her first one which was also brilliant! Finished it in 3 days not even normally a reader but I couldn't put this down! Definitely recommend and can't wait for the third!"
- UK

"There are many adaptations about the life of Queen Elizabeth I, but with this new book, Leah Toole still manages to convey new aspects and interesting information for me in an exciting way. My recommendation: have tissues ready…"
- Germany

"Having read 'The Saddest Princess', I knew I had to read this as soon as it came out & I was not disappointed. Even though I am an avid Tudor fan & pride myself on my knowledge of the Tudors & queen Elizabeth, I was still surprised to learn some of new things in the book. As always, Leah Toole wrote this magnificently & I could feel myself tearing up throughout at the life Elizabeth had. Incredible story telling from Leah Toole."
- UK

"This book is so good, whether you love Tudor History, like me, or know very little about it. This book covered decades but was fast paced, never lingering too long on a point in history. 100% a page turner. The author made you feel sympathy for Elizabeth on one page, and had you hating her the next. It was brilliant. I can't wait for the third instalment of this series."
- Canada

Also by Leah Toole

The Tudor Heirs Series

I – The Saddest Princess
...
II – The Haunted Queen
...
IV – The Forgotten Prince

I dedicate this book to
all the children who have been
manipulated and used by those who should
have had their best interests at heart.
Know that you're not alone.

Prologue:

January 1547

  I have always known I would one day become King of England. After all, was that not precisely why I was born?
My father had had his fair share of the disappointments of women – not only through his wives' failures, but also from the useless gender of his two eldest children.
I was what he had always prayed for.
A son.
A male heir to further the Tudor line and to keep England under the safe protection of a *man*!
It's no wonder, really, that my father had been so aggressive in his pursuit of me, for the idea of leaving the country behind to a woman…well the very thought of it alone twists my stomach!
Or perhaps it's the news of my father's death that is to blame for my sudden onset of nausea…for in an instant, and at the age of just nine-years-old, I am no longer simply Henry VIII's beloved Prince. But King Edward VI of England!
This day has approached far sooner than I had imagined it would. And, in truth, I *had* hoped my father would have had another son yet.
His last marriage to queen Catherine Parr had given me hope that I would not be his sole male successor. To have had someone I could've relied upon to follow me in case –
No.
I mustn't think that way.
My father has died. And I am his only surviving male heir.
That is all that matters.
I know my duty. I know what I must do.

And though I cannot, yet, envision myself in the future with a wife by my side, I am sure I shall manage to plant my seed into whomever she may be when the time is right.

I may not be successful with my first, or even with my second wife. But if my father had taught me anything, it was that *women* were to blame for a man's inability to reproduce.

For we – men! – were created in the image of God Himself.

And Henry VIII and I, as kings, would not be at fault for any of our shortcomings.

No, I am not worried.

July 1553
Greenwich Palace, London

God was punishing me.

What other reason could there be for this cruel twist of fate?

I had been born Henry VIII's most precious jewel. The county's future. And the Tudor dynasty's salvation.

My birth had marked my father's most joyous success after decades of failures.

And yet, unbeknownst to everyone, it had also sealed the Tudors' fate. For though I had been born a boy, I had not been as perfect as my father had hoped or believed.

Though of course he had never known.

And neither had anyone else.

Except for *him*...

A coughing fit consumes me suddenly, my throat feeling raw and my chest heavy from the constant hacking up of black fluid over the last few weeks.

A servant boy steps forward from out of nowhere and wipes my chin with a silk handkerchief – since I am too weak to do it myself – before disappearing once again into the shadows.

As I settle back against my feather cushions, I cannot help but breathe a laugh at the irony of it all: the lengths to which my father went to sire a male heir, only for that male heir to be – well...me.

Though...I had *planned* to do my duty. I had planned it all out. Every single detail.

And yet I do find myself wondering if I would have been able to go through with it.

I look up at the beautifully carved ceiling of Tudor roses in each panel, and sigh as I feel another coughing fit beginning to brew at the base of my throat. And as I hack up some more tarry sputum, I allow myself to admit what I already know.

That, for me, it was no longer a question as to whether I lived or died, for there was only dying left for me to do.
And that, when it comes to what would have happened had I endured? It no longer mattered...
As to whether I would have done my duty?
Well, I guess we will never know.
Because I never got to live.

Chapter 1

20th May 1536
Wolf Hall, Wiltshire

"What say you, Jane?"
King Henry VIII was towering over a pale-faced Jane Seymour, his sweaty hands holding onto hers, engulfing them with his firm grip.
It had been but one day since the former queen's beheading.
Jane, who had served as a lady-in-waiting to Anne Boleyn, had been as stunned as the rest of the country at the queen's public execution.
Granted, king Henry had arranged for a French swordsman to do the deed, rather than a common axeman. But the fact that he ordered – and then persisted – with the beheading at all had been alarming. No one had believed that he would *actually* go through with it.
After all, the king hadn't even organised a coffin for his second wife, her poor decapitated body being stuffed into an old arrow chest instead.
Jane had not cared much for her former mistress, but even she could acknowledge that Anne Boleyn's treatment in her final days had been cruel and callous.
And now king Henry wished to marry her. Plain Jane Seymour. She could not have been more different to the former queen if she had tried.
Jane knew she was no beauty. She had been told as much her entire life.
And yet, for some reason, the King of England had begun pursuing her in secret months ago, even before his former queen had irked him so.

Did he love her?

Jane was not sure. But she knew what her family expected of her in this situation, for one did not simply turn down an offer of marriage from the king!

Her feet tingled nonetheless at the question, the blood rushing through her body in a distinct fight or flight response.

She realised then that Henry's jaw had set tightly and that his thick hands had begun to tremble as she continued on in silence, his grip tightening to the point of pain.

But Jane knew it was not fear of rejection that made him so tense, but rather the aggravation of waiting.

Jane had noticed over the years that the king was not a patient man, much less so now that he was in his forties and yet to attain a surviving male heir, despite being married twice before.

"I accept," Jane replied coyly then, just as she knew he appreciated, after years of having been married to the hot-headed and opinionated Anne Boleyn.

With a victorious guffaw Henry let go of her slender hands, and when he turned and called to summon his servants, Jane released a slow breath to steady her nerves. She rubbed her hands together to bring back the circulation he had cut off with his grip as her father and two of her brothers emerged from the other room.

The eldest of the two, Edward, entered straight-backed and with a confidence he had boasted since boyhood, a fox-like smile pulling at the corners of his mouth.

Edward nodded once at her from across the room as the king approached their father and clapped him heartily on the shoulder, and she noticed how her father recoiled slightly at her new husband-to-be's touch. But he quickly applied a cheery grin to his face, knowing all too well that if the king wanted to marry a lady, neither her father nor anyone would have a say against it.

Jane glanced down at her hands, still clasped before her. And she thought of how she could settle her father's mind about this new turn of events for their family.

But the thought swiftly flew from her mind as she uncurled her fingers like the petals of a blooming flower, the tingling in her palms continuing to vex her. And as she opened her pale hands, she noticed her fingers were marked with red raw indentations, caused by Henry VIII's many-ringed hands as he had clenched hers tightly, completely unaware that his passion was quite literally carving chunks right out of her.

"Why her, Henry?" Charles Brandon, Henry VIII's oldest friend and member of the Privy Council, asked on their return to London later that day, "Out of all the princesses of Europe, all the beautiful ladies of England, why choose this plain Catholic?"

Henry waved his hand and scoffed as he sat heavily on his great warhorse, "What do you care if she is beautiful or not?"

Charles frowned, his old friend confusing him, since a woman's beauty was of course directly linked to her fertility.

Everyone knew that!

But he did not reply, and they continued on in silence for a while.

"You are not aware then?" the king said after a moment, breaking the silence.

Charles raised his dark eyebrows, "Whatever I ought to have noticed has escaped me, Your Majesty," he said.

Henry laughed, his belly jerking up and down as it spilled over the front of his black horse's saddle.

"Her mother," the king said simply, to which Charles narrowed his brown eyes, still unable to comprehend.

"She bore her husband *six* healthy sons, Charles! Six!"
Finally, it all made sense to Charles Brandon, and he nodded slowly, a small smile playing upon his thin lips.

"So it is not love, then?" Charles asked, hoping to understand, "You have chosen the lady for her mother's fertility, hoping she would be as successful in the production of sons."
The aging king grinned, flashing his yellow teeth, "Precisely."

30th May
Whitehall Palace

The wedding took place but eleven days after the former queen's execution, and yet the king had managed to arrange for Anne Boleyn's falcon emblems to be hurriedly replaced with Jane's own personal crest of a phoenix rising from a castle among flames, with Tudor roses of white and red sprouting from the fruitful land.

Anne's initials, too, had been removed and replaced with Jane's. King Henry's 'H' now brandished as intertwined with Jane's 'J' in a great display of unification.

Though much preparation had been hastily made to ensure no trace was left of Henry's former wife on the day that he would wed another, it did not make Jane feel at ease. And all it succeeded in doing was making her realise just how effortlessly women could be replaced.

But Jane was not scared. She did not fear the king as Anne had done, for Jane believed with every fibre of her being that this was God's plan.

Jane knew of her shortcomings. She was not pretty, nor witty, nor accomplished. Her family name held no significant value since her father's scandal many years prior, when he had seduced his own son's wife...

And yet, somehow, the King of England wished to marry her.

Her! A woman of twenty-seven years, with no value to him as a bride.

What reason could there possibly be other than that it was divinely guided? God must have chosen her to steer the king and England back to its former glory. To return it to a Catholic country under the loving protection of the Pope.

With that knowledge, Jane vowed to do what she could with her new position as Queen. It was the least she could do to thank God for this gift He was laying upon her. For with this new glory, Jane Seymour would be able to erase her family's tainted reputation caused by her father, as well as follow in the *true* queen, Katherine of Aragon's, footsteps and to be a loyal and obedient wife to the king.

After all, as Jane's motto stated, she was 'bound to obey and serve'.

And though she hoped to right a few wrongs along the way, Jane certainly wished to do just that.

June 1536

As a Catholic, queen Jane had always believed that the king's marriage to Anne Boleyn had not been lawful, and that the child produced from their union to be illegitimate.

Not only had they conceived Elizabeth outside of wedlock, but Jane – as well as all Catholics – had never truly accepted the king's annulment from Katherine of Aragon. And so therefore, when he had wed Anne Boleyn, he had still been married to queen Katherine in the eyes of God.

Though most of the country had signed the oath proclaiming king Henry and Anne Boleyn's marriage as lawful and the children produced from it legitimate, it did not alter what many knew in their hearts to be true: that Katherine of Aragon was the true queen, and that their daughter Mary was the king's only legitimate child.

Because of this, when Jane accepted the king's proposal, she had decided to take it upon herself to try to reconcile her new husband with his eldest daughter.

She had heard of the vile treatment the young Princess Mary had endured throughout the years since her mother's banishment from court. The threats to her life, the dissolution of her household, it all brought on a bought of nausea to the new queen, and it made her think of her husband's other daughter, the little Elizabeth. With her mother's beheading and accusation of adultery, there was no doubt in Jane's mind that the girl would likely face similar shunning from her father as Mary had suffered.

She shook her head with sadness for the poor child. No one deserved such treatment, no matter the sins of their mother.

But her disgust over Mary's mistreatment over the years had opened her eyes as to what kind of stepmother she wanted to be, and she knew that no matter how she felt about little Elizabeth's legitimacy, she would never stoop so low as to incite cruelty onto the child.

Nevertheless, Elizabeth *was* a bastard in the eyes of God. Whether the reformation had allowed for her legitimacy or not, in the eyes of the Catholics she had been born outside of holy matrimony.

And so Jane decided that, for now at least, she would concentrate on reuniting her husband with his legitimate daughter. The one born to his true wife, Katherine of Aragon.

For the time being, little Elizabeth was safe and cared for. And until she was in danger, there would be no need to intervene in her young life.

Mary, however, would no doubt need much love to be poured into her to regain her footing within this world, after so many years of neglect and abuse.

And now that Mary had finally signed the Oath of Supremacy, after years of having refused and been threatened with death by her father, she would surely be allowed to return to court life. Jane would help her to heal along the way. She would be honoured to.

All she had to do now, was try to persuade her husband to invite Mary back to court.

Mary had not been back a month before tragedy struck, and news that the king's only surviving son had died, rocked the kingdom to its core.

Henry Fitzroy had been born during his marriage to Katherine of Aragon, when the king had taken the young Bessie Blount as his mistress over seventeen years ago. She had conceived and borne the king a healthy son, a son who had very nearly been legitimised and betrothed to Henry's daughter, Mary. The Pope had even granted him papal dispensation, allowing for the half-siblings' incestuous union if only Henry had given up his pursuit of Anne Boleyn.

Henry had refused the Pope's offer of course, his quest of Anne having, at the time, seemed like a better option to the king than the promise of a legitimized boy by his mistress. And in truth, everyone had known that the people of England would never have accepted his bastard boy as king – legitimized or not.

"Am I cursed?" the king asked Charles Brandon then, his head in his hands as he sat upon his gold throne at the end of the great hall, "Must all my children die?"

Charles found Henry alone in the hall, his footsteps echoing as he made his approach towards the king.

The empty hall felt cold and dreary, its usually merry atmosphere having died along with the king's happiness.

While the teenaged Henry Fitzroy had been illegitimate, he had been the king's only son to have surpassed the dangerous years of infancy, and had therefore been living proof that Henry VIII could in fact produce a healthy male heir.

"There is still hope, Your Majesty," Charles Brandon replied tactfully, "Henry, you have a new, young wife. She will bear you many more sons, God willing!"

But even as Charles spoke the words, he was not entirely certain if he believed them anymore. Henry had spent over two decades in pursuit for a male successor, and it was becoming increasingly clear that perhaps a surviving son was not in God's plan for England's king.

Later that day, as Henry and his new queen, Jane Seymour, lay naked beneath the king's silk sheets in his royal bed, shrouded in the darkness of the night, the king opened up about the boy he had just lost.

As Henry spoke without pause, his words flowing freely in the darkness, Jane's mind wandered and she began to contemplate what her own future as Queen of England would look like, and the pressures that came with the new title.

Two queens had previously failed to give the king a son and heir, two queens that he'd had shunned or killed…and while she wanted to believe that the king loved her, his son's death gave Jane a new perspective on Henry's desperation for a male heir.

Jane shifted, suddenly uncomfortable in the king's embrace and she wished then that he would leave so that she could kneel at her private prie-deux and pray to God for a swift conception of a healthy son.

For she knew – given the king's track record with surviving sons – that she would be praying for a miracle.

July 1536

Queen Jane had regretfully commenced her courses, signifying that another month – two since their wedded union – had now passed without the hope of a male heir.

She could tell, by the way the king looked at her with disappointment and disgust, that he was hugely displeased, and he openly displayed this to her in the way he ogled other ladies of the court without a care to her feelings.

Ladies who were considerably more attractive and younger than she.

Jane had tried not to take it to heart, knowing that the loss of his son would still be weighing heavily upon his conscience. And yet it did not stop a low-burning flame of fear to flicker within her, quivering to-and-fro with every sidelong glance of distaste he threw her way.

But while her womb remained empty, she knew what she must do.

"My love," she said, as she glanced up at him from beneath her lashes, her voice smooth like melted butter, "Forgive my boldness but I wish to ask you to consider something."

They were seated within the king's private chamber, the table filled with many marvellous dishes of roasted pig, sweetmeats, sugared grapes and more, the king's appetite having increased significantly since his near-fatal fall at a jousting match some years prior.

Henry looked up from his plate of food before him.

"What is it?" he asked as he chewed loudly, and Jane wondered just how she had never before noticed his ability to be so unappealing.

She reached a hand across the table and touched his forearm, stroking it lovingly as she spoke.

"I know the loss of your son weighs heavily on your heart and your mind," she smiled at him sympathetically, "his death leaves you without a son, and though he was illegitimate I am certain the people would have accepted him as king if it had been your wish."

She did not believe her own words, knowing that the people would have absolutely *not* accepted a low-born bastard boy as king, whether he had been legitimised by the Pope or not. But she watched as Henry took a large gulp of wine, blinking away tears as he drank, and she was glad to have managed to be tactful in her delivery.

Now was the moment to make her proposal clear to him.

"Perhaps, now that he is gone," she continued carefully, "we should look to your other children to succeed you?"

He did not reply and continued to simply stuff more sweetmeats into his mouth.

"I suggest this only to keep your throne secure until I have borne you sons," Jane continued then in an effort to explain herself, "The lady Mary is loved by many, and if you reinstate her as heir apparent, it would keep Your Majesty from –"

"Jane," he said, cutting her off. But his voice was calm.

Too calm.

It sent a shiver down Jane's back.

"Don't ever speak to me of matters such as these again," he said.

His response made no sense to Jane.

She had been confident that he would have seen the logic in her suggestion. And in her inability to comprehend, she replied.

"But, Your Majesty –"

"Are you mad, woman!?" he shouted suddenly as he interrupted her, "I said: do not *ever* speak of this again! Do you understand?"

Jane stared back at her husband, her face completely drained of colour, but she nodded.

"Yes, Your Majesty," she mumbled and resumed eating, the meat and bread tasting like dust in her mouth.

"In any case," the king said then, his rage gone in an instant, "you should be focusing on the continuation of *our* line, not that of dead women's bastard children."

Jane felt sick. His sudden hostility had utterly horrified her, and for the first time since he had begun courting her over a year ago, Jane gave the queens who had come before her a sympathetic thought.

Perhaps Jane had been fooled.

Chapter 2

September 1536

Though the king continued displeased with his newest bride for her failure to conceive an heir, to the outside world, Henry was very much besotted.

He favoured his new wife's family above any other – much as he had done with his former wife's family – and created one of her brothers, Edward, Viscount Beauchamp of Hache. With this new title, the family was granted lands and manors in Wiltshire, as well as a large annual income.

The Seymour family name was on the"rise'

All plain Jane had to do, was cement her position as queen, and conceive a male heir to maintain – or indeed to incite – the king's love. For though it appeared to the world that he was madly in love, Jane had learned the truth, and behind closed doors Henry made it perfectly clear how little he thought of her.

"Does he still visit your bedchamber?" said the queen's brother Edward unblinkingly, as though it were the most usual of discussions.

Jane blushed, this was not an appropriate topic of conversation to have for a sister and her brother. As well as an inappropriate question to ask one's queen.

But she nodded in response, and her brother inhaled deeply as he thought.

"It has been only a few months," he said, "There is time yet."

Jane continued to stare blindly ahead as she squeezed her hands together tightly in her lap.

She did not want to admit it to her brother, but the king had not been a gentle husband of late.

Compared to their wedding night, where Henry had been considerate and tender, now Jane would be lucky to receive so much as a quick peck on the lips before he pulled his hose down to his ankles and inserted himself inside her.

There was no more tenderness to their lovemaking. And each month that she failed to conceive, only fuelled the anger Henry felt towards her.

But last night had been different.

In the most humiliating way.

Jane had been certain she had finally been blessed with a child, so much so that when her courses had been two days late, she had been considering telling her husband the happy news.

But that night she had awoken with a terrible cramp, and her bedsheets beneath her had been soiled with blood, her courses making a late appearance with a vengeance.

Henry had been informed, as he would be for the rest of Jane's days – the king knowing any and all of his wife's business – and that very night, as her ladies were helping her change from her bloodied nightshift, the king entered the queen's bedchamber, dismissing everyone but his wife.

Jane had stood naked by the fire, her arms wrapped around herself subconsciously as Henry made his way towards her.

"I am so sorry –" she mumbled, but the rage in his eyes flashed brightly.

He had reached up a hand as if to caress her cheek, and for an instant Jane had thought that perhaps he had come to console her.

But then he grabbed a handful of her blond hair, which had been plaited into a loose braid for the night, and pulled her down to kneel before him.

Jane had called out in pain and fallen to her knees, trembling with fear as he had ripped the buttons of his hose open and wrenched out his manhood.

Jane had looked up at him with tears in her eyes, "My lord?" she had asked, puzzled as to what he expected of her.

Without a word, the king had grabbed her by the hair once more and shoved himself into her unsuspecting mouth, groaning immediately, his power over her in that moment arousing him far more than the sexual act itself.

Jane's eyes shot open wide as he had forced himself into her, and as he moved back and forth inside her mouth, tears began to stream down her face.

She had very nearly vomited due to the feeling of him at the back of her throat, and for a moment she thought she would, when suddenly he withdrew himself from her and ejaculated over her naked chest and neck.

Jane had whimpered in horror, her tears free flowing as her husband cried out in pleasure before her. And as she folded herself up as small as she could, Henry stuffed his exhausted manhood back into his trousers and sighed.

"That ought to teach you to use my seed sparingly when I am good enough to squirt it *into* you."

And with those parting words, he had turned and walked out the door, leaving Jane a broken mess on the floor.

Jane's mind returned to the present then when her brother shook her gently by the shoulder, calling her name.

She raised her gaze to meet Edward's then, blinking as though she had just woken from a dream.

"Are you unwell, sister?" the new Viscount asked.

Jane shook her head, "No, Edward. I am well," she lied, "I only wish to do my duty by my family and my king."

Edward nodded approvingly, "You are doing just that, sister. Just keep doing what you're doing. The king is clearly madly in love with you."

Jane smiled up at her brother and nodded, and she wondered how no one else could see that behind her smile, she was already dead inside.

October 1536

King Henry was enraged.
Not only had he and his wife – the wife whose mother had borne *six* male heirs for *her* husband – been married for six months without so much as a hint of conception, but now he was having to deal with an uprising in the north of England.

"Who are their leaders?" Henry asked his Privy Council as he absentmindedly picked at a hole in the wooden council table.

"Robert Aske is one of them, Your Grace," Thomas Cromwell, Henry VIII's right-hand man and chief minister said, "He is a lawyer. And a Catholic of course. He and their army wish to overturn the government and Your Majesty's reforms."

"Your reforms," Charles Brandon, Henry's closest friend mumbled, to which Cromwell shot him a shrewd glance.
But Henry paid them no attention, their hate for one another being old news and of little interest to the king.

"Their numbers?" Henry asked brusquely as he shifted his large frame in his great, gold throne.
Cromwell riffled through his papers, "There are many, my king," he said, then produced the letter he was looking for, "Thousands, this newest report says. And growing by the hour."

"What, *specifically*, has caused this?" the king asked, hoping to understand his people's discontent.
Cromwell swallowed, knowing that he had played a large part in what was causing the northerner's unrest.

"It seems their displeasure was sparked off by the dissolution of Louth Abbey," Cromwell explained sombrely, "Three thousand men marched from Louth to Caistor, and trouble erupted. Two men, including the Bishop of Lincoln, were murdered by the rebels. They have written up a list of grievances which include the dissolution of the religious houses."

What Cromwell had failed to tell the king, was that the Catholic rebels' list had also mentioned their grievance against the Protestant Thomas Cromwell's rise in power.

But he went on, "At the moment they are ten-thousand men strong, and they demand a reply from Your Majesty in regard to discussing the points on their list of demands."

Henry looked up from the table and silence befell the council chamber for a moment.

He leaned back in his throne, his fingers intertwined as he rested his hands upon his increasingly rounded belly.

"I will send a messenger," the king said finally.

"To discuss their demands, my lord?" Charles asked, dumbfounded, "Surely not!"

"Of course not," Henry replied, "To do so would mean the removal of my own chief minister from my Privy Council," and he shot Cromwell an amused look.

Thomas Cromwell breathed a nervous laugh, his eyes wide as he realised the king had been more aware of the goings on of the Northern Rebellion than he had previously let on. And had no doubt been testing his loyalty to share everything with his king.

Cromwell would have to be more careful in the future, for to lose the king's love would be fatal.

"We will send a warning," the king continued, "Charles, as Duke of Suffolk your forces ought to be enough to squash their numbers if I wished it, would it not?"

Charles Brandon nodded.

"Then write it up, Cromwell," Henry ordered, turning to look upon his favourite, "Word it however you please. Just make sure those traitors understand that to continue to stand against their king means putting their lives in direct danger. Make sure to threaten them with arrest and death. I will not have the common Catholic folk telling *me* what they believe I can or cannot do."

The threat alone did not scare off all of the rebels, and Charles Brandon Duke of Suffolk was later sent to the north with the instruction to destroy, burn and kill any man, woman and child he and his army encountered as part of the rebellion.
But the numbers Charles' army faced upon arrival was not the mere ten-thousand they had been warned about, but thirty-thousand, leaving Charles outnumbered.
Their leader Robert Aske, however, chose to negotiate, and he commanded his army of disgruntled peasants to lay down their arms so that he and the Duke of Suffolk could attempt to settle the dispute without bloodshed.
Over the course of the following days, king Henry and Robert Aske negotiated, with Charles Brandon as the middleman.
But Aske would not back down from his demands, which ranged from a decrease in food tax, to the reestablishment of religious houses.
"We cannot give into these demands," Cromwell told his king one evening as he and his queen sat at the dining table in the queen's chambers, "If we do so with this rebellion, then there is no knowing what future rebellions will think to petition from you, their sovereign lord! If we do not stop them soon, they may gain support from other Catholic countries and mount an invasion to overthrow you."
Jane looked up carefully from her plate of pheasant.
Henry was rubbing his forehead in thought, the truth behind Cromwell's words falling heavily upon his shoulders, "Tell them I shall give into all their demands," he mumbled.

"Your Majesty!" Cromwell gasped, but Jane sighed with relief at her husband's words to spare the Catholic folk.

"This could be the end of all your hard work!" Cromwell went on, "To give into Catholic demands –"

"Damn it, Thomas!" Henry interrupted loudly as he met his advisor's horrified look, "I am sick to death of this back and forth! *Tell them* the king shall meet their demands. *Tell them* I shall pardon them all. We shall *tell them* whatever they damn well want to hear."

Cromwell bowed and scurried from the room, to which Jane couldn't help but smile, for she and her husband's right-hand man did not see eye-to-eye. Though no one would ever have noticed, queen Jane being too softspoken to mention anything aloud.

"You are a good king," Jane commented once they were alone again, unaware of her husband's true plans for the rebels. She offered him a brief smile, "To offer the rebels pardon is very noble."

Henry stuffed a forkful of meat into his mouth and chewed loudly, "Don't, Jane," he muttered without looking at her.

Jane blinked, "I only mean to show my support in your decision-making," she explained. But Henry only sighed.

"Jane," he said then after a moment of silence, his tone low, and yet somehow it sounded more threatening than if he had shouted, "I suggest you do not involve yourself in kingly matters."

Jane swallowed her pheasant along with her growing fear.

Then Henry reached over and plucked a chunk of meat from her plate, his eyes never straying from hers.

"Or need I remind you what happened to the last woman who meddled in my affairs?"

*

King Henry's offer of pardon, and the promise of acceptance of their demands, had worked. And before long the thirty-thousand rebels began to return to their homes.

Only a few hundred, as well as their leaders, Robert Aske, Thomas Darcy and Robert Constable, remained. And it was then that the Duke of Suffolk was able to suppress the much smaller group of rebels, his army of several thousand overpowering them easily.

And they were all executed for their crimes against the crown.

December 1536

Four days before the Christmastide, queen Jane received news that her beloved father, Sir John Seymour, had died.

Sir John had long preferred a life outside of the public eye, his own daughter Jane not even being able to remember if this had always been the case or whether it had developed after the scandal.

The scandal where he had seduced his own son, Edward's, wife and very likely fathered his own grandchildren…

But despite his failures, Jane had still loved him. He had been a flawed father figure, no doubt, but Jane could not believe that he had erred in his paternal ways out of calculated malice. He had simply been a man of poor choices. And Jane had forgiven him many years ago.

His sons, however, had not. And so, when his death was announced so close to the Christmastide, the queen's three surviving brothers found excuses in not being able to attend their own father's funeral due to the political importance the Christmastide held for new members of the nobility.

"May I be granted permission to attend?" queen Jane asked her king once she had heard that hardly anyone would be present for her father's funeral.

Henry did not look up from the documents he was perusing.
His Secretary of State, Thomas Cromwell, was leaning over the king's shoulder, pointing out a piece of information on the parchment, and mumbling into the king's ear as though the queen had not even spoken.
Jane shifted her weight onto her other foot as she continued to stand, unnoticed, before the two great men.
She knew better than to ask her question again.
She also knew that she *had* been heard, and that her husband would answer her when he deemed it necessary. Since he was, of course, dealing with more important matters than the whining of lesser women.
Finally, Henry looked up and blinked, as though he had forgotten she was there.
But Jane knew he hadn't forgotten. He was merely continuing his maltreatment of her as he had done every day since her first bleed after their wedding.

"Oh, Jane," he said, raising an eyebrow and sighing, as though she were asking a great favour of him, and not just the permission to bid farewell to her father.

"Your Majesty," Jane said as she bobbed him a pretty curtsy, hoping to soften his emotion towards her.
She met his blue-eyed gaze, hoping to find some compassion in them.

"You do know," he said as Thomas Cromwell took a step back into the shadows where Jane had noticed he liked it best, "As queen, you are not permitted to attend funerals."
Jane looked down at her hands as she replied softly, "I had hoped you would be so magnanimous as to reconsider? Just this one time?" then she looked up at her husband with tears in her eyes, "He was my father."
Henry sighed and turned to stare into the lit fireplace, and Jane's heart skipped to think her king was considering her plea.

Then he returned his icy gaze onto her, "I shall not," he said, "A royal's presence at such an occasion would bring into question their own mortality. I cannot risk that while you have neglected to grant me an heir."

Jane looked down again, like a child being scolded for her failures. But she nodded her head.

"I understand, my lord," she mumbled.

And, being the good and loyal wife she hoped to be, Jane truly did understand.

For just like the regal Katherine of Aragon before her, Jane knew that only *she* was to blame for her own misfortune.

March 1537

"I fear for my sister, Your Grace," the Lady Mary admitted as she and her new stepmother walked leisurely through the palace gardens.

The Spring showers had ceased for the day after a week of constant downpour, and the gardens were beginning to dry in the warm sun. It was the perfect occasion to escape the confinements of the castle walls and to voice concerns aloud without the risk of being eavesdropped on.

"Since her mother's death I have not been able to see Elizabeth at Hatfield," Mary continued, "And judging by my own mistreatment over the years, I fear my father will not care to make sure she is comfortable."

"She is illegitimate," Jane replied in defence of her husband, somewhat fearful that he had eyes and ears even within the safety of trustworthy company.

Mary nodded, "But, in my father's eyes, so am I," she replied, "And yet, here I am."

Jane sighed, "It took the king many years to accept you back in his presence. And you had to do things you did not wish to do.

Give it time. One day, God willing, the king may very well return little Elizabeth into favour."

Mary looked down at the cobbled path they were walking, her mouth downturned in sadness as she thought of her beloved little sister, shunned and forgotten just as Mary had been.

Jane had noticed that, while she and her husband's eldest daughter were but eight years apart, Mary looked many years older than her twenty-one years – her father's abuse having etched deep worry lines into his daughter's face.

But Jane thought the young lady pretty, nonetheless.

Not a beauty by any means. But certainly pretty enough for the queen to wonder why no noble lord or prince had snapped her up as a wife yet.

But of course, her father was to blame for that, his public slandering of his first marriage's legality causing the poor Mary to be deemed as an illegitimate bastard to many within Europe. Catholics believed otherwise, however. Just as Jane did.

And she hoped that, with the newest development within her own marriage, that Mary – as well as little Elizabeth – would be restored into their father's favour very soon.

"I have news," the queen said then as she interlocked her arm with her stepdaughter's, a smile on her face which she hoped would steer Mary's mind away from the unfortunate things she could not change.

"What news, Your Grace?" Mary asked, a small smile tugging at the corners of her mouth.

Jane looked behind them and waved her hand at the many ladies-in-waiting that trailed behind. Mary followed her gaze and watched as her ladies, Frances and Cecily, as well as the queen's four curtsied and took several steps back.

Then Mary and Jane resumed their slow stroll through the neatly trimmed hedgerows.

"God has answered my prayers," Jane said quietly, her face aglow with joy as she searched her stepdaughter's eyes for a shimmer of understanding.

Mary's pale blue eyes widened, "He has?!" she breathed, immediately knowing of what she spoke.

Jane nodded, "I have not told the king yet," she confessed, "But I am certain. I have missed two courses."

Mary grinned, "I am happy for you," she said. And she meant it with all her heart.

Mary had seen how her father had continued to dote on his wife in public. She, as well as the rest of the court, had witnessed just how attentive, gentle, and kind he was whenever they were together at events, banquets and gatherings.

But Mary knew from her own experiences how her father could be when he did not get his way. And there was no doubt in her mind that, in private, the king would likely have been anything but loving to his wife while she had not conceived during these past few months.

But by the grace of God, queen Jane was finally with child.

Mary felt an intense wave of relief washing over her as she realised the stepmother she had grown to love would likely be spared from either of the king's previous wives' terrible fates. But at the same time, she felt a knot of dread forming in her stomach at the prospect of this child being a boy.

It was, of course, the very thing her father wished for the most: a male heir to succeed him…

But though Mary very much wanted her father to put an end to this incessant search for an heir, she continued to hope that he would one day look upon her and remember her own worth. That *she* would be just as good a successor as any son.

But today was not that day. And Mary knew that it would likely never come to pass. Not after everything he had done to rid himself of her mother, Katherine of Aragon.

And yet it did not stop her from praying for it.

But despite Mary's personal wishes, she was greatly pleased for queen Jane.

She embraced her tightly, just as she knew she ought to at such news. And all the while, Mary tried desperately to quieten the screaming thoughts in her mind that willed the baby be born just another useless girl.

May 1537

King Henry – and therefore the rest of the court – was overjoyed at the news that the queen was *finally* with child.

He had, shortly before her joyous announcement, been considering other ladies as her replacement. Anne Bassett, the stepdaughter of the 1st Viscount Lisle, Arthur Plantagenet, having been an interesting choice for a wife.

But the queen had been able to conceive after all, God be praised.

Henry's two previous wives had conceived immediately upon their unions. And so he knew, of course, that it had been nothing wrong with *him* when Jane had not immediately been with child.

But his prayers had been answered, and he would make sure the whole of England would hear of this glorious news so that they could all be assured that their king was still as strong and capable as when he had first been crowned nearly thirty years ago.

"The babe is strong, my lord," queen Jane said as she and her husband sat side by side at the long dining table in the great hall.

"'He'," the king replied, "He is strong."

Jane smiled faintly and nodded.

The court was merry. Music played freely from all the corners of the hall as many lords and ladies danced. Chatter and laughter was heard above the music as other courtiers continued eating heartily or draining their cups of wine before smacking a kiss upon their loved one's unsuspecting lips.

Jane felt at ease for the first time since her wedded union with the king over a year ago, and she sat back against her throne to observe the court's glee in full swing.

Just then, as she had shifted into a more comfortable position upon her cushioned throne, Jane felt a soft thumping from within her belly.

"Oh," she said as she looked down at her bump, her hands hovering over it with uncertainty.

"What is it?!" the king asked then, his voice gruff with horror that yet another child would be born too soon.

But then the queen felt it again, a soft tapping in the dome of her belly, and she looked up at Henry with a smile on her face.

"It is the baby," she said, "*He* is showing me just how strong he is," and she took her husband's big hand and gently placed it where she felt the little movements.

Henry looked into Jane's shining grey eyes then as he felt a little wave underneath his hand. And in that moment, he thought that Jane had never looked more beautiful.

27th May 1537

In celebration for the queen's conception and announcement of the strong quickenings she was feeling, Henry arranged for many celebrations to occur across the country.

Te Deum was sung in St. Paul's Cathedral in London.

The Bishop of Worchester gave a speech before the House of Lords and the House of Commons, asking them to pray that the queen continue fruitful, and to pray to God that He would send them a Prince.

At night, bonfires were lit, and wine – paid for by the crown – was enjoyed by the people in the streets throughout the country. And the celebrations continued for many days, the people of England revelling in this new hope for an heir to the throne. One they had been waiting for for twenty-eight years.

July 1537

In public, as well as in private, Henry showered Jane with gifts, compliments and affection, and Jane could finally experience what it really felt like to be truly loved by Henry VIII.

She had seen glimpses of his charming nature when he had secretly courted her for a year before Anne Boleyn's execution. She had received many love letters and poems from him in that year and shared hurried, whispered confessions of lust in the shadows. Their wedding night had been sweet and tender, and she had had the distinct impression that her life as Henry's wife would be nothing short of magical.

But since their wedding night, Jane had not seen the caring man she had married, and instead known only that other side to Henry that she never wished to see again. She had thought that side reserved for wives who had somehow betrayed him – Jane only ever having witnessed his fiery temper directed towards Katherine of Aragon, who he believed had deceived him, and Anne Boleyn who had committed adultery against him.

But it seemed that his patience had run out much quicker with Jane once he had had her, and she had often wondered if perhaps the love he had confessed for her many a time when it had been forbidden was nothing more than a clever ruse for ladies to go weak in the knees.

It had worked on her, naïve as she was in the arts of men.
But God had been watching over her. And He had finally granted her a child to appease the king's growing distaste.
All that was left to do now, was to continue to pray to the Lord Almighty that this child would be Henry's long-awaited male heir. And if God was watching over her as she believed He was, then she would surely never have to bear witness to her husband's terrifying displeasure again.

Chapter 3

8th October 1537
Hampton Court Palace, London

  Jane had bid the court farewell three weeks prior and travelled to Hampton Court Palace to begin her confinement, where she would spend the following month in quiet and darkness.
The king, having known many losses with his two previous wives, had ordered for Jane to remain on bedrest upon her arrival at the Palace, which the queen and her household had obeyed without question.
The queen had watched from her four-posted bed as her ladies moved quietly about the chamber, draping large tapestries over all the windows to block out any light.
The midwives believed that, during the final month of confinement, it was imperative that mothers remain in a womb-like space as they awaited the arrival of the baby.
And the arrival of this baby would be no different. For its safety was of the utmost importance.
The birthing chamber remained dark and quiet as the days and nights passed without much ado.
And yet, all the while, as Jane lay quietly in her bed, her mind was loud with anxious thoughts.
Jane knew how much was riding on the safe delivery of her child. Of the safe delivery of a *male* child.
Her family name was at stake. Her reputation, as well as her brothers'.
But most importantly, her continuation as queen.
If she could deliver a healthy male heir, her duty as the king's wife would be complete, and he would likely dote on her for

the rest of their days for having given him what he had long been searching for.

Her continued position as a Catholic queen in this crumbling country would be detrimental to the potential return to the true faith, one that her husband only abandoned in his vile pursuit of her predecessor.

Jane shifted uncomfortably in her great bed then as her thoughts turned ugly, and she ran a hand over her large belly.

She shook her head clear of those thoughts. This was not the time for such dark thinking.

And so, she turned her mind to God instead, and she prayed silently that He would protect her from this perilous journey ahead.

Little did she know that, while she prayed for salvation and prosperity, her babe was beginning its descent, and that a long and troublesome labour would be ahead of her.

9th October 1537

Jane Seymour awoke from a short slumber to a cramping in her lower back, and within moments, all Hell broke loose.

The midwives were called to bring in the small pallet bed where Jane would give birth to spare the royal mattress. They placed this at the foot of the great four-posted bed and helped the labouring queen onto it gently.

The queen's ladies gathered around her, some whispering words of encouragement while others prayed or read the bible aloud.

"Where is the pain, Your Grace?" one midwife asked, to which Jane pointed at her lower back.

The midwife nodded and lifted the queen's nightshift before rubbing an ointment onto her back.

Jane's nose crinkled at the offensive smell, "What is it?" she asked.

The midwife breathed a laugh, "It's a remedy to soothe your pain, Your Majesty. The smell will be the eel liver."

At the revelation, the queen's ladies inched a little further from their queen, and Jane's lip twitched, thinking she ought to have refrained from admitting to a pain until it had become a little more unbearable. For surely, things would only get far worse before they got better.

Jane had been right.

Her tightenings continued throughout the night, the pains travelling from her lower back to her bump, and all the way down her left leg. And by this point, no amount of pain-relieving ointment was helping.

"Breathe, Your Grace," one of the older midwives coaxed, "In, out, in, out."

Jane was standing at the foot of the bed, bent forward at what looked like an awkward angle as she held onto the bedposts, but she claimed it was the only way she felt marginally comfortable.

She breathed in and out as her midwife demonstrated, never allowing her sweet demeanour to slip as she wished for nothing more than to slap the old woman's face, the breathing doing nothing to aid her pain or the babe's swift arrival.

Jane's leg was beginning to throb as she stood, the weight of her swollen body causing her much discomfort as the night passed by in a blur of pain and useless mumblings from her midwives.

Three days and three nights passed without progression other than Jane's waters breaking in the early hours of the morning of the third day.

By now, exhausted and weak from her many hours of pushing without the arrival of her baby, Jane could do nothing but lay back in the pillows of her royal bed.

The pallet bed that had been brought in for the birth had been removed and forgotten, the higher comforts of her feather bed having called to her as her strength had begun to fail after the first twenty-four hours of labour.

"You must keep pushing, Your Majesty," the eldest midwife insisted to the ashen queen.

But when Jane could do nothing but shake her head slightly in reply, the midwife turned from Jane's bedside and hurried out the door.

The midwife walked hastily through the palace hallways until she found a messenger waiting idly in the courtyard.

"Send an urgent message to the king and his physician," the midwife said, "A decision will soon need to be made."

"The mother is likely to die," a physician told the pale-faced King of England as he received news of the queen's labouring development. Or rather, lack thereof.

"If the messenger's account is accurate and the queen's strength is depleted without a sign of the child, it is probable she and the babe, both, will perish," the physician continued as Henry dropped his gaze and stared blindly at the floor before him.

"The midwives have suggested *caedare,* Your Majesty," the messenger added then.

"It is not yet time for that," the king's physician snapped back at the young messenger boy beside him, "The queen is not yet dead."

"Will it save the child?" Henry interjected then, his mind racing to find any way of gaining a live babe from this colossal failing from his wife.

Even if it is another girl?
The thought nearly knocked the king from his throne as the uncertainty of life continued to taunt him.
But it mattered not. The choice was clear.
One way or another, someone would die if the labour did not progress. Naturally or unnaturally.
At least with this method, Henry would have half a chance of obtaining his long-awaited heir.
  "Cut him out."

12th October 1537

  It was two o'clock in the morning when the messenger arrived back at Hampton Court Palace to deliver the queen's death sentence in favour of the life within her.
But by the time he made his way up the staircase to inform the midwives of their king's decision, the young man was relieved to hear the delightful cries of a newborn baby.
Queen Jane had finally delivered, one of the younger midwives having taken matters into her own hands and making one careful cut into the queen's birthing passage to allow the child to be born with one great, final push.
By the grace of God, the precious child had been born a boy, and the young messenger was made to swiftly turn on his heel to tell the king and country the most amazing news.
Queen Jane lay back among the feather pillows, her face grey and clammy from the fatigue and pain of a long and arduous labour.
But it had all been worth it, she thought, for the miracle that now lay safely in her arms.

  At the break of dawn, every parish church throughout London tolled their bells for the safe delivery of a Prince of the realm.

Two thousand gunshots were fired off the Tower of London to mark this glorious day, and the people danced and sung in the streets.

And all the while, Queen Jane was recovering from the ordeal of childbed, none the wiser that her husband had ordered she be sacrificed but a few hours earlier.

"How do you feel, Your Grace?" said the midwife who had likely saved her life by administering the cut down below that had released her son from inside her.

Jane was sitting propped up against fresh pillows on her newly mattressed royal bed, her brand-new baby boy wrapped up in swaddling and sleeping soundly in his wetnurse's arms as he fed.

"I feel well," Jane said as she continued to watch her perfect little creation.

The midwife curtsied and left her queen's bedside, glad to have aided in this most significant event.

"Here," Jane said to the wetnurse then as she held out her arms, "I wish to hold him."

The plump wetnurse removed the babe from her breast and handed him gently to his mother. Then she curtsied and left the chambers.

Once Jane was finally alone with her infant, she allowed herself to relax.

The throbbing ache in her left leg had not ceased since the very beginning of her labour three days ago. She had thought it would have passed by now, no doubt being some natural pain brought on by the pressure and strain of birthing a child.

And yet it persisted, despite the rest of her pains having eased shortly after the prince's arrival.

Jane looked down into her sleeping baby's peaceful face and inhaled deeply.

This pain, too, shall pass, she told herself. *It has been but eight hours since the traumatic ordeal, surely my body simply needs time to heal.*
And she made herself believe it. Even as the pain between her legs subsided the following day, and the ache in her leg continued to pulsate uncomfortably beneath her skin.

"The queen's midwives have reported tragic news, Your Majesty," the king's physician said.
It had been nine days since the miraculous birth of Henry's favoured child. Since his son's birth he had organised many banquets and masquerades in celebration, giving speeches dedicated to his most beloved wife as she recovered well in confinement.
But on the morning of the tenth day, his queen had taken a turn for the worse, the midwives believing her sudden turn to be directly linked to the incision she had endured to her genitalia during the birth.
"Is it childbed fever?" Henry asked then, visibly trembling in fear for his adored wife's life.
The physician swallowed and took a step towards his king, wringing his hands together as he considered how best to broach the subject.
"The queen's wound, while it was healing well to begin with, has become infected," he said slowly, deliberating each word as he spoke it, "But that is not the news I wish to discuss with you."
Henry's head snapped up, a frown etched between his red brows, "Speak, dammit!"
The old man licked his lips, "The queen is strong. I have no doubt she will survive this turn of events. She is sitting up and eating well and is even continuing to sign letters announcing the birth of the Prince of Wales."

"Then what is this tragic news you speak of?" Henry thundered then as he rose from his seat by the fire.

The physician looked over his shoulder at the open door of the king's chamber, manned by two guards.

The king followed his gaze, then snapped his fingers at the guards, "Out!" he shouted, to which the two men bowed their heads and quit the room, closing the door behind them.

The king and his physician were alone and silent for a moment, the only sound coming from the great hearth beside them as the flames cracked and licked at the logs inside it.

"The midwives have examined the queen," the physician said quietly as he leaned closer to the king, though they continued alone, "They have concluded the lady's labour to have affected her birthing chamber."

The king blinked, his lip curled up in disgust, "Why must I hear of this unpleasant development?"

"Because, my lord, it is my expert opinion that the lady's troubles in ejecting the prince from her womb, has directly affected her ability to conceive again. Which means a potential spare heir, or even princesses, by your legal wife are out of the question."

Finally, it all made sense, and Henry's eyebrows shot up in understanding.

He nodded his head slowly then as he raised his hand up to his thinning copper hair and raked his fingers through it.

Then he breathed a small laugh and shook his head.

"Your Majesty?" the physician said, watching as the king walked slowly away from him and into the shadows.

"Women," was all the king said in response, and the physician looked after him in confusion.

"It seems none of them can birth a Prince right."

"What will you do?" Charles Brandon asked.

Henry and his life-long friend sat side by side by the fireplace in the king's chamber later that same day. The room was engulfed in shadows save for the one slice of light from the fire which danced over their features. But it did nothing to erase the dark look on the king's face.

"She is useless now," he replied, staring at the flames as they snaked around the charred logs.

Charles Brandon did not respond. Instead, he watched the king think, aware from the look in his eyes that he had already decided to be rid of his wife.

For Charles had seen that same look twice before.

24th October 1537
Hampton Court Palace

The incision between Jane's legs was causing her some discomfort.

But it was nothing compared to the throbbing pain that continued to pulsate angrily in her leg.

It felt warm to the touch, the skin on the back of her calf glowing red from whatever ailment possessed her.

But still, she could not bring herself to mention it to her midwives or even her ladies.

Jane knew that she had to show the world that her recovery was going well, and show her husband that while her labour had been a struggle, she would recuperate swiftly and without complaint.

But today she could not contain her discomfort, and in the early hours of the morning, upon waking feeling nauseous and lightheaded, queen Jane called for her ladies.

They wrapped their mistress in furs to warm her while a servant girl was sent to fetch Jane her favourite foods.

Throughout the following hours, her nausea subsided slightly, and Jane was able to doze a little in the hopes of finally regaining her full strength.

But she was awoken just before midday when she heard trumpets sounding outside, signalling the arrival of her husband and king.

"Ladies!" Jane called, "Help me up and wipe my brow. I must look my best."

She ignored the young women's sideways glances at each other which suggested the queen was far from looking anywhere near presentable, nevermind her best. But they did as she bid them, their efforts doing little to hide her ashen complexion and heavy-lidded gaze.

When the doors to her bedchamber opened and the king was announced, Jane's stomach dropped to see the blank look on his face. One which, though he wore a smile upon his lips, was meant to signal only to her that she had somehow displeased him.

And she couldn't possibly understand how.

"My most beloved wife!" he called as he hurried towards her and knelt beside her bed.

He took her hand in his and kissed her knuckles, to which Jane forced a smile as she knew she should, for the benefit of those watching this charade.

She wondered how many people he was fooling with this show of affection. Wasn't it clear to everyone that his eyes held no life when he looked upon her?

"Your Majesty," she mumbled, already exhausted by his presence, "Our son –"

"Oh, he is marvellous!" Henry interrupted loudly, "And you, my queen, are a wonder to behold!"

Jane's smile twitched slightly, and she noticed his gaze narrowing as they both recognized each other's façade.

But then Henry turned to the guards and ladies behind him.

"I wish to be alone with my wife," he said, ordering them to leave.

Suddenly Jane's breath caught in her chest.

She tore her hand free from his as everyone exited her chambers, and held it flat between her breasts, the heaviness in her chest feeling suddenly like it was squeezing her from within.

"Henry," she whimpered quietly, her voice straining to be heard as she pleaded for help.

At the sound of her voice, the king turned back to his wife, the click of the door behind them confirming their privacy.

"Jane," he said, a soft smile playing upon his lips which felt eerily out of place to Jane as she tried to tell him that she was suddenly struggling to breathe.

But then he lifted his hand to wipe her hair from her clammy forehead, "You did your duty, sweet Jane," he whispered as he leant over her with one great hand on either side of her head.

"And for that, I am, and always will be, eternally grateful."

Jane searched his eyes for understanding of what she could have possibly done since birthing his long-awaited son to now, where all she wanted to do was recover so that she might bear him *more* sons.

But the ache in her chest was growing stronger, and she writhed under her furs, her hand grabbing fistfuls of her nightshift.

Henry saw her struggling and smiled, "There's nowhere to go," he said, misinterpreting her efforts to breathe as trying to get away from him.

Suddenly the king reached over and grabbed a feather pillow from beside her head and crushed it down over her face.

Jane squealed once before the pillow came down, and then her cries were drowned under the heavy weight of Henry's grasp.

She thrashed her legs as hard as she could, but it did nothing to even budge Henry from his comfortable sitting position beside his wife, his firm grip continuing to crush the life right out of her.

Little did he know that as he covered her face with the feather pillow, a blood clot had dislodged from Jane's leg and embedded itself into her lung.

And though Jane continued to struggle, she was in that moment being suffocated from within as well as out.

"I left her to sleep," king Henry said as he buried his face in his hands the following day.

The physicians before him wrung their hands together and hung their heads, "It appears she succumbed to her infection, Your Grace."

At that, Henry wailed, his shoulders shaking with the distress of the news.

He knew, of course, that his wife had not died of perpetual fever as his physicians were suggesting, though he thanked his luck that she had indeed developed a small infection in the incision to her birthing canal.

Henry shuddered. Even just the thought of Jane's destroyed genitalia sent a shiver of disgust over the king, and he knew that with this one swift act, he had spared himself another messy separation.

Not only that, but to have gotten rid of Jane publicly through an annulment or beheading as he had done his other two wives, would have meant the question of his son's legitimacy.

And *that* must never come into dispute.

But of course, now it never would. And with this new development, queen Jane would be remembered eternally as the angel who had given her life to grant her king his most desired heir.

Following Jane Seymour's death just twelve days after the birth of England's prince, the country went into mourning for the sweet-natured queen.

Her eldest stepdaughter, Mary, who had grown to love and respect her stepmother, was inconsolable. She locked herself away in her chambers and wept for days, not only for herself, but also for her new baby brother who would grow up never to know his own mother.

Queen Jane's loss was felt all over the country, for her purity and kind-heartedness had become common knowledge among the people. And the fact that the gentle queen had given her life to deliver the king his long-awaited son only made her death so much more tragic.

In place of the king, who traditionally could not attend any funeral, Mary was appointed Chief Mourner at the queen's interment in his stead.

And so, while Jane's coffin was being transported to Windsor on a hearse drawn by a horse draped in black, and the country mourned her passing, Mary found herself wondering if her father would ever take another wife.

Would marriage even be on the forefront of his mind now that he had attained his precious male heir?

As the coffin was being lifted off the horse-drawn hearse and brought into St. George's Chapel, the Lady Mary could not stop the tears from falling, and her mind fell to her brand-new baby brother once again, and the emptiness with which his life had begun.

Mary could only imagine how his heart would forever be searching for someone he had never even known. The misery of it all dawned on Mary, and it pained her that her two young siblings had learned at such young ages that even to be born into royalty could not protect your heart from breaking.

April 1538
Greenwich Palace, London

England was weak.
Though the king *finally* had his heir thriving in the nursery, he was once again unwed and therefore without the prospect of potentially producing any spares, which – as the second born son to his own royal parents – he knew first hand to be critical for the security of the Tudor line.
However, even with that in mind, Henry could not bring himself to consider another lady – whether for personal or political gain – for the guilt of Jane's loss was still too much to bear.
The king had locked himself away upon Jane's death.
Three months of utter solitude where he had made a show of allowing entry to no one but his fool Will Sommers, to entertain him during the days as he tried to drown his guilt with wine.
But in the nights Henry would secretly send for ladies to entertain him in other ways, admitting them through the secret passageway hidden behind a panel of his bedchambers.
No one but his closest friend, Charles Brandon, knew of these ladies. For Henry had to be perceived to be in despondent mourning for his beloved queen.
It was not intense despair that Henry felt at the death of his third wife – his actions to provoke her demise instigating no sadness within him. But as the weeks had passed, her demise began to incite an intense guilt which he could not seem to shake, despite believing to his core that it had been the only logical thing to do.
No matter how many jokes Will Sommers told, or how many cups of wine he drank, or how many women he bedded, the heaviness of Henry's guilt continued to weigh on him.

And now, six months later, the king could not even bring himself to visit his precious son for more than a few moments without Jane's face flashing before his mind's eye.

As though her ghost would forever taint the miracle that was his son's life.

But his inability to bond with his treasured son was not the only issue the king faced of late.

An old wound from a past jousting accident had become inflamed and painful some days earlier before bursting open one night as he had slept. An extraordinary amount of infected fluid and blood had seeped from the wound, rendering the king's bedsheets sullied beyond repair.

Henry's physicians had cleaned the wound and given him a remedy for the pain, but after several days the wound had not yet begun to heal and as a result Henry's irritation was never far behind even the mildest of inconveniences.

"Why should I concern myself with that girl when she is likely not even my own!?" the king bellowed at his eldest daughter, Mary, then as she stood before him in the great hall.

Mary could not bring herself to reply right away, for a pungent stench struck her as she stood before the king, and she realised that the old wound on his leg must have burst once again.

"The lady Elizabeth may have been born illegitimate," Mary eventually replied tactfully, trying desperately to breathe through her mouth, "but there is no denying that she is your daughter, father. She is such a clever and witty young girl, with many interests beyond her age. Not to mention her fiery red hair. All characteristics she has undoubtedly received from you."

Mary had come to plead her father to take pity on his daughter by his second wife, Anne Boleyn.

The poor girl, after having been shunned by Henry since her mother's swift beheading, had been living in poverty and left utterly forgotten at her household in Hertfordshire.

Two years had passed since her mother had been accused of treason. Two years in which the little girl had, of course, grown and was therefore in need of new attire. Attire which her father the king ought to grant her, surely, since it was one of the most basic of human needs.

Besides, the poor child herself had done nothing to offend the king, other than to be borne by her mother, the Great Whore.

Could the king really hold that against his old flesh and blood? Henry rubbed his hand over his face and groaned.

"I am told Elizabeth is clever and wise beyond her years," the king replied, "*that* I can admit she has from me," he paused then as he sighed heavily, narrowing his pale blue eyes in thought.

"I grant you your request, Mary," the king announced after a moment, as though it were the most generous gift, "I shall have bolts of cloth sent to the girl's household. The servants can make of it what they will."

Mary smiled tightly and curtsied, "I thank Your Majesty for your generosity," she said before hurrying away in an effort to escape the rotting smell that clung to the ageing king.

Chapter 4

June 1539
Richmond Palace, Surrey

Though Prince Edward was as motherless as his two royal sisters, he would never quite understand their suffering.
Despite being but two-years-old, the young prince knew that he was the most precious baby in all of England, and though he rarely saw his majestic father, he was cared for especially well by his many governesses.
Each day had a carefully planned out routine, much the same as the day before. But baby Edward didn't mind, for he rather enjoyed being doted on every minute of every day.
His favourite time of day was when the servants would clean the palace, dozens of them on their hands and knees scrubbing the floors and walls to ensure the prince would never encounter even a scrap of dirt.
He did not notice their pain, of course. At two-years-old he understood little of worldly misfortune. But he enjoyed watching their repetitive up and down of the scrubbing brushes all the same, as though it were a methodical performance they would enact just for him.
But the most special days were when his beloved sister, Mary, would come to visit.
Prince Edward's chest would fill with a warm fuzzy feeling when she made her way through the palace gates, a feeling he would have reserved only for his mother had she lived.
But Mary was that person for Edward, the one who he hoped to see when he woke up in the mornings, and the one who he believed was the most gracious being on God's good earth.

She showered him with gifts whenever she came to visit, a silver rattle or a hand carved wooden horse. But what Edward cherished even above her glorious gifts, were her loving looks and gentle caresses.

As the Prince of Wales and future King of England, Edward was no stranger to people touching him. His entire life he had been passed from one wetnurse or governess to another, never alone even while he slept. But Mary's gentle touch felt different. She was warm and kind, smiling whenever he did the most mundane of things.

And though Prince Edward knew that she was not his mother, for his royal mother had sacrificed herself to give him life, Mary would always be at the very centre of Edward's heart.

For she, even above his own father, seemed to truly care about his happiness.

August 1539
Greenwich Palace, London

"What of the duchess of Milan, or Mary of Hungary?" king Henry asked.

The thrice married King of England had been without a wife for almost two years, and with the country now facing a potential invasion from their greatest enemies, Spain and France, the people were in desperate need of a new alliance.

Cromwell looked down at the floor, uncomfortable with having to be the bearer of bad news, "It appears neither is in favour of a match with Your Majesty," he said.

Henry's face went red with humiliation and anger, and Cromwell continued quickly, "But I have a proposition for Your Majesty, if you would permit me to continue?"

Henry clenched his jaw but sat down and waved his hand for Cromwell to resume.

"I would like to suggest a match with Germany," Cromwell announced, "Specifically, the princess Anne of Cleves. It would strengthen England against the new alliance between France and Spain, and I hear the princess Anne is very well spoken and considered a beauty."

The men of the council watched as their king rubbed his fat chin slowly in thought.

Though Cromwell knew this proposition would indeed help to strengthen the country, his suggestion of the princess of Cleves as a wife for the king stemmed mainly from a personal gain, for he believed that a union with a devout Protestant princess from a deeply Lutheran family would give England the push it needed to fully reform from the Catholic faith, which Cromwell abhorred above all else.

Henry met Cromwell's gaze; his lips pursed in thought.

"Have them bring me a portrait of the lady," the king simply said, his voice utterly emotionless, for he had very much desired the duchess of Milan since seeing her portrait some weeks prior.

"Your Majesty," Cromwell bowed and resumed his seat, eager to move on before the king asked for more details regarding the declined proposals, the young duchess of Milan's refusal having been anything but gentle.

If I had two heads, I would happily put one at the disposal of the King of England. Alas I have but one.

It was becoming increasingly clear to Henry's Secretary of State that to find a foreign princess of which he had no absolute power over – and could therefore not simply force into marriage – would be tricky to obtain.

Luckily for Cromwell, the princess Anne of Cleve's brother was keen to marry her off to expand his own fortunes, and though the lady herself may not be so inclined to accept this union, her brother lorded over her in all matters since their father's death.

All that was left to do to achieve this advantageous merger for Cromwell's Protestant cause, was to get the old king to agree with this choice of wife.

And if the threat of war wasn't enough to push the king into acceptance, perhaps Cromwell would have to pay the king's painter, Hans Holbein, a friendly visit.

December 1539
Deal, Kent

Princess Anne of Cleves arrived in England after several weeks of travel, at the head of a grand retinue comprising of two-hundred-and-sixty attendants with two-hundred-and-thirty horses.

Strong winds had delayed her departure from Calais, but upon her arrival on English soil, she and her household were met by the king's guards and Sir Thomas Chaney.

Sir Thomas led the royal household to Deal Castle so that they may rest before continuing their journey towards London.

Anne was glad to have a few days to compose herself before she was to meet her future husband, for the journey across Europe and the choppy sea had left her quite fatigued and no doubt looking dishevelled.

"It has been arranged for Your Grace to meet the king at a formal reception at Greenwich Palace," Sir Thomas Chaney told the German-born princess as they rode at a leisurely walk through the town of Deal.

The princess smiled kindly and bowed her head in recognition that he had spoken but unfortunately, she was unable to comprehend all that was being said.

She turned her head towards the German ambassador, Christopher Mont, who quickly translated under his breath.

The fair princess nodded.

"Ich brauche dringend mehr Englischunterricht, damit ich mit dem Konig kommunizieren kann," the princess told her ambassador then, who swiftly turned his horse around to arrange for the lady's English lessons to commence as soon as her household had rested, as she had requested.

The following day, despite not being fully recovered, Anne of Cleves and her household continued their journey towards London and made their way to Rochester.
Once there, the lady had been told, she would be met by the king's advisor, Charles Brandon Duke of Suffolk and his wife, as well as the Bishop of Chichester and various lords and ladies. She braced herself for arrival.
Though she had been born to John III, Duke of Cleves, and his noble wife Maria, Duchess of Julich-Berg, and was therefore familiar with royal customs, she was not well versed on *English* customs.
Anne had been educated well enough. She knew how to read and write well…in German.
Her parents had never deemed it important for her to learn English as a child, since she was betrothed to marry the heir of Antoine, the Duke of Lorraine's son, when she was just a little girl.
But that betrothal had been deemed unofficial and been cancelled some four years prior. Ever since then, her brother – who was now head of their House as their late father's eldest son – had been trying to be rid of her at his most profitable convenience – a *king's* offer in marriage being at the very top of his list of fortunes. Higher perhaps than he had ever considered his sister of being able to achieve.
Her brother had played the negotiator for a time, having heard that king Henry enjoyed the chase even more so perhaps than the bedding.

But after just a few months of back and forth, her brother had agreed to marry her off to the king no other noble lady in Europe had wanted.

In the short time since the signing of her wedding contract, Anne had not had the chance to learn much of the English language, though she had applied herself at any given opportunity that she had.

She clung onto the few sentences she had learned over the last few weeks as she and her household made their way through Rochester's gates.

She held her head high and her back straight as she sighted the many lords and ladies who had come to greet her, hoping to calm the storm that thundered inside her, as though she were still out upon the choppy sea that had brought her here.

Bishop's Palace, Rochester

"We shall rest here a few days, Your Grace, before continuing to Greenwich Palace," Charles Brandon told Anne of Cleves later that day once she and her household had settled themselves into her newest temporary lodgings.

To the noble lady's surprise, Rochester Palace had not been in particularly good condition – according to the king's advisor – to accommodate her household, its proximity to the muddy shores causing it to crumble due to excessive dampness.

Instead, they were housed in Bishop's Palace in Rochester, which was more suitable for a lady of her station.

Anne accepted her accommodations with all the grace and grandeur of a lady born to be an English queen, when in fact she had not been prepared for this role whatsoever.

*

"I *vin*," the princess Anne declared the following day as she laid down her cards face up, a wide smile spread across her face.

Katherine Brandon, the Duchess of Suffolk, looked down at the princess' cards, her mouth hanging open in feigned irritation.

"Well done, Your Grace," she said slowly, to allow the lady to understand her, "You win," she added, as a form of gentle correction.

"I win," Anne repeated, to which Katherine nodded approvingly.

The German-born princess' grasp of the English language had developed well in the two days she had remained in Bishop's Palace, though it would take many more weeks and months to reach her full extent of understanding.

Her grasp of popular English card games, however, had taken but a few hours to absorb, already beating Katherine on most occasions.

"Again?" Katherine Brandon asked as she picked up the deck and shuffled.

"Maybe...Chess?" Anne replied slowly in her heavy German accent.

Katherine smiled before snapping her fingers, "Bring the chess table," she ordered one of Anne's servants.

Anne looked swiftly to her servant as he stared back wide-eyed.

"*Schach,*" she whispered to him, aware that he would likely not know what the lady had asked of him.

He bowed his head and hurried away, and Anne sighed happily to herself.

Knowing that she was not alone on this strange journey – her household, too, having yet to learn so much about their new surroundings – gave her some relief. But she was well aware that those born beneath her in rank might take even longer than she to learn, her lessons being to no one's advantage but her own.

And so, conscious of this imbalance of fortune, princess Anne would always be glad to help in any way she could to make this frightening situation a little less disconcerting for those who had travelled here with her.

January 1540

As Henry VIII was en route to meet his new bride in disguise, he could hardly contain his excitement.

He had very much liked the portrait Hans Holbein had painted of her, showing a fair woman with green eyes and a small mouth. Her nose seemed a little on the large side, but he had not been deterred by that one minor flaw, for he could tell by the penetrating look in the paint's eyes that she would be a docile and caring wife. One who would hopefully give him many sons. Sons with a claim to her brother's lands in the West of Germany. Henry jolted atop his horse then as a vivid memory of Jane Seymour flashed before him, her ashen body lying lifelessly in the royal bed she had died in.

The royal bed she had been killed in, a voice in Henry's mind chimed in.

A voice so much like that of his second wife's, Anne Boleyn...

But he shook his mind free of those memories and raised his head high. Today was not a day to remember previous wives' failures, but a day to celebrate the bright future ahead.

Soon he shall meet his new fair maiden. And they will undoubtedly be blissfully wed for many years to come.

"A guest, Your Grace," Princess Anne of Cleves' lady-in-waiting said in German as she took her place behind her mistress.

Anne turned from the window she had been gazing out of, a ready smile on her lips as she wondered who would visit her so rashly and without previous announcement.

A tall man entered with five companions spread out behind him, advancing directly towards her.

She nodded her head in greeting and opened her mouth to speak when suddenly the tall man embraced her warmly, and brazenly planted a wet kiss upon her lips.

Anne, understandably shocked and confused, wrestled free from his embrace, her green eyes wide with surprise.

For a moment she only stared at him bewilderedly while the man grinned at her, satisfied with her reaction of displeasure at the idea of an embrace from someone other than her future husband.

Judging his disguise to have fooled her completely, he was satisfied to believe that she would be a loyal wife.

Henry – the stranger – bowed at the waist and presented her with a gift.

"A New Year's Eve gift for you, my lady," he said.

The Princess took the box carefully from his outstretched hand and passed it to her lady-in-waiting behind her.

"*Zank* you," Anne said quietly, continuing unsure as to who this gentleman could be and what gave him the right to kiss her so candidly when surely, he and the whole of England should know that she is to be wed to the King of England himself!

In that moment it became clear to the regal Anne of Cleves.

This man before her was either playing a horrid trick on her, or this was in fact *him*. The King of England.

For whom else would be so bold as to kiss her if he were not her own future husband?

She regarded him with narrowed eyes as he straightened himself from his bow and offered her a yellow-toothed smile.

Anne returned his smile warily, unsure if she should encourage that kind of tomfoolery.

She returned her gaze to the window beside them then, silently considering her next words, since she was not yet entirely sure that this *was* indeed her betrothed.

The princess could sense that the man before her wished to speak but was likely just as bemused as she at this strange encounter – though it was *he* who imposed so unexpectedly upon her.

From the corner of her eye, she could see the five men behind him shifting uncomfortably, so she turned to face them once more when the tall man bowed at the waist yet again.

"Your Grace," he said, an impish smile on his face and a twinkle in his eye that solidified Anne's belief that this was indeed the King of England in playful disguise.

She felt her cheeks blush at the intense eye contact from him then, and she lowered her gaze, a small smile tugging at the corners of her lips.

Later that same day, as Anne of Cleves and her household entered the hall to attend dinner, she was surprised to see the tall man from earlier sitting at the top table, this time dressed in a black velvet shirt and hose stitched with gold thread, and a great feather cap upon his head.

This was – without a doubt – King Henry VIII of England.

Immediately upon noticing him, Anne dipped a deep curtsy, her ladies behind her following suit.

Henry regarded her.

She was dressed in a pale green dress cut in the German fashion, her sleeves ballooning at the upper arms and shoulders, and the cut of the skirt much higher at the waist than was fashionable in England.

Her hair, though tucked underneath her hood, appeared to be of dark-blond colour based on the colour of her eyebrows, which Henry noticed were thin and lightly arched.

He liked her appearance very much, though he certainly would prefer her in a more English attire.

Or no attire at all.

The thought popped in his head before he could stop it, and he felt a rousing in his hose which he hoped to extinguish very soon on their wedding night.

"My beautiful bride!" the king bellowed as he made his way towards her with outstretched arms.

Anne blushed and smiled, "Your Majesty," she said slowly, her German accent prominent, "It *vas* you…"

Henry laughed, a deep throaty laugh, "It was I indeed, my lady," he replied, "Did I fool you?"

Anne nodded, as she assumed he would have wanted.

They made their way towards the dining table which was filled with many exquisite dishes.

Musicians started playing in the corner, and chatter began to fill the hall as Anne's ladies and other members of her household took their seats at various wooden tables.

The king and his future queen sat side by side at the centre of the long table at the head of the little banquet, occasionally stealing glances at one another as Henry shovelled fistfuls of food into his mouth.

Anne watched him carefully, her eating habits being of an entirely different nature to that of the English king. And as she elegantly ate one small mouthful at a time with the help of a two-pronged fork, she was taken aback at how unruly the king beside her was conducting himself at the dinner table.

But the English had different standards of manners, she reminded herself, and soon enough she would be used to their ways.

Once dinner was concluded, Henry beckoned his new bride to a games table by the roaring fire.

"I should like to get to know my future queen a little better," the king said, and Anne noticed he was purposefully speaking a little slower so that she would understand.

She offered him a pretty smile, appreciating his consideration of her. Then she sat opposite him at a cards table as he began to shuffle.

"Have you learned *Primero* since arriving in my country?" the king asked.

Anne smiled again, "It is my…favourite."

Henry returned her smile, detecting that her cheeks blushed lightly when she looked at him. He bowed his head in admiration that she had learned the English game and dealt out the cards.

Glad to have noticed that her answer had pleased the king, Anne was excited to show off her skills in the hopes of gaining more approval from her fiancé.

They sat by the warm fire all evening, talking little but playing hand after hand of cards, all of which the foreign princess won. By the time the fire had died down to nothing but embers, Anne continued to be warmed by her own sense of pride at having showcased her ability to learn about the king's English ways – of language *and* games – so quickly.

Blinded by her own excitement to please her future husband however, she had not noticed that – while their conversation had been little at the beginning of the evening – it had become utterly non-existent by the end of the final game.

Henry sat back in his seat with a *humph* then, having been beaten for the eighth time in a row by the more inexperienced and younger foreign lady.

And he did not like the feeling of failure it evoked in him.

Not even a little bit.

"I shall retire," the king said then as he stood up in one swift motion.
Anne stood too, "Retire?" she asked, unsure of the word.
Henry waved his hand about, "You know. Leave. To bed."
Anne smiled, unaware of his change in mood, "Ah, yes," she said and then curtsied, "*Gute Nacht.*"
Henry only raised his eyebrows in recognition that she had spoken. Then he turned on his heel and left.

The following morning, much to Anne's surprise, the king entered the hall where she and her ladies had been breakfasting, with an entirely different aura about him.
His red brows were etched tightly together, his lips pursed in such a way that made Anne think he had smelled something foul.
He made his way towards them as Anne and her ladies rose from their seats and curtsied before him.
"Your Majesty," she said, "Good morning."
She looked up at him from beneath her lashes with a charming smile, and Henry softened a little, though she had stumped him the eve before.
Perhaps she had not meant to humiliate him when she had beaten him eight consecutive times in a row, Henry thought.
She continued as pretty as ever, her demeanour reminding him very much of his first wife in her youth, when she had been young, gentle and eager to please.
Perhaps he ought to give this foreign princess another chance to redeem herself.
"Good morning," he replied, and he took her hand and kissed her knuckles, his frown evaporating right before the princess' eyes.
The unwitting princess felt butterflies in her stomach at the idea that her mere presence had soothed His Majesty's temper so –

unaware that it had been irked by her to begin with – and her cheeks blushed fervently at the king's touch.

True, he was not a young man. Anne had noticed right away when they had met the day before, that he must be at least twice her age. He was not as handsome as she had been made to believe either, from the stories she had been told on her journey to England. He had manners she would never have expected in a noble king, his eating habits having shocked her at the dinner table the night before. And sometimes, when he shifted his leg in his seat, a pungent smell would waft about him.

But despite those things, Anne had been pleased after their unorthodox meeting when he had brazenly kissed her in disguise. She had seen a shine in his eyes upon their meeting that had given her hope, and now, upon seeing his anger dissipate at the sight of her, Anne was beginning to believe that perhaps *she* would be the wife to calm king Henry's infamous temper.

For three hours, the king and his bride had been sitting by the fire in complete silence, when Charles Brandon walked in to inform Henry of their schedule for departure.

The king was bent over the chess table as he stared wildly at the checkmate status before him, the princess Anne sitting back triumphantly in her seat.

Charles regarded the image before him with wide eyes, fully aware – as Henry's lifelong friend – that even a minor defeat such as that of an unimportant game, would irk the king beyond common understanding.

Charles had known, from many years of observing the king during their youth, that to lose was not in Henry's realm of acceptance. Even if it were a loss over a simple game of chess… But had anyone thought to tell his new bride to submit to feigning losses?

It would appear not.

Anne turned a beaming face to Charles when she noticed his entrance. It seemed the poor fool was utterly unaware of the detrimental fracture she had inflicted upon her future husband's already-frail ego.

"Your Majesty," Charles said, hoping to break the king's angry stare from the chess table, "The horses are ready."

Henry blinked then as if waking from a trance and he inhaled deeply, his eyes closed in an effort to compose himself.

"Let's go," he said then, and he rose from his seat as fluidly as the rotting ulcer on his leg allowed.

"Go?" Anne of Cleves repeated, "Your Majesty is leaving?"

Henry froze but he did not turn to look at her, and his face was as deadpan as though the lady were nothing more than a mere peasant in the streets.

When Charles realised the king would not be offering his bride a response, he took a step forward, "The king has urgent matters to attend to. But Your Grace will commence your travels to Greenwich Palace on the morrow."

Anne nodded slowly, having understood only half of what the kind Duke of Suffolk had said.

She turned to her betrothed and offered a curtsy in farewell, a bright smile spread across her friendly face, "Your Majesty."

The princess had expected for him to kiss her hand once again, or to have at least bowed his head in gentlemanly parting.

And so, when the King of England quit the room without so much as a glance in her direction, Anne of Cleves was left wondering if she had somehow, without her knowledge, committed a mortal error against the king.

"I like her not!" king Henry bellowed at Sir Thomas Cromwell upon his arrival back at Greenwich Palace later that same day.

"She is nothing like her painting, and she is as dull as a kitchen maid!"

Henry had thought about his new bride the whole journey back to London, and he had had nothing but a bad taste in his mouth ever since.

It mattered little to Henry that he, in truth, found her extremely pleasing on the eye, and that he had enjoyed her calming company greatly during his visit. But her inability to submit to him even for a simple game did not sit right with him.

Yet he could never admit to such fragile self-worth.

Whatever distaste he felt towards her stemmed from her own failures, of course.

As a woman, she should know to bow down to her husband in all things…

Thomas Cromwell shook where he stood, wide-eyed before his king, "But the diplomatic ties with the Duchy of Cleves –"

"I like her not!" Henry interrupted his Secretary of State, "I do not wish for this union to progress! Find me another wife. One who would be deserving of a benevolent king such as I!"

The following day, Anne of Cleves and her household arrived at Greenwich Palace where she would be formally presented to the king, as had been originally planned.

She wore a plain dress of black damask and a dark veil which covered her face as well as her hood.

The princess was announced by the king's usher, and Henry's eldest daughter the Lady Mary couldn't help but notice that her father sat straight-backed and sour faced on his throne upon the princess' announcement.

When Anne of Cleves had her veil removed and was formally presented to the king, Mary noticed that – though she was not extremely beautiful – she was not as ugly as recent rumours would have had her believe.

Her face was round like the moon, but Mary noted that her awfully styled hood did not help the matter either, and despite her round face, Mary noticed that her eyes were a beautiful shade of green.

Mary wondered then, as the princess Anne curtsied elegantly – what exactly had happened during the king's brief visit at Rochester to warrant such a cold reception from him. For by looking at the princess herself, Mary could not say with certainty that her appearance would have been the real problem, as her father had been complaining about since his return.

She looked away from the round-faced princess and glanced quickly at her father as he welcomed her cooly to his court.

His expression was one of utter disappointment, and Mary suddenly felt extremely sorry for the poor young lady standing awkwardly before them.

Though they may have nothing in common as far as language or religion, Mary offered the lady a reassuring smile, in hopes of making her feel more at ease.

Anne of Cleves returned her kind smile and then looked down at the ground before her, and in that moment, Mary saw something in her eyes.

Something Mary had seen far too often in her own eyes throughout the years: Fear.

Chapter 5

February 1540

The new Queen of England had been married for over a month, but she was yet to know her husband intimately.

"Every night," Queen Anne said as she confided in her new ladies in broken English, "the king comes to my bedchamber and tries to consummate the marriage. But he cannot…"

Her ladies looked at one another, their brows furrowed with worry.

The youngest of her ladies, a pretty girl named Kathryn with big almond-shaped eyes, took a seat beside her mistress.

"Have you tried to…" she said as she waved a hand in the air between them, suggesting the queen try to somehow aid her husband with his troubles.

Anne of Cleves frowned, unaware of what her young lady was referring to.

As a noble lady – and a virgin at that – Anne of Cleves was not very knowledgeable of the acts of passion. She had been warned of the pain she would have to endure the first time she lay with her husband, but that it was a woman's duty to give herself to him uncomplainingly.

Was a woman supposed to do something she had not been forewarned about?

Upon their wedded union before God a month prior, the king and queen had been escorted with all due ceremony to the marriage bed which – to the new queen's horror – had been carved with all manner of phallic symbols.

It had been blessed by the Archbishop of Canterbury and scattered lavishly with rose petals. It had been the perfect place to consummate their royal marriage.

Anne had lain down on her back as she had been told to do.
Then her new husband had crawled on top of her with nothing but their thin nightshifts between them. He had lifted her nightshift with what Anne believed to have been resentment, before stuffing his hand in between them and vigorously pumping on his limp manhood. She had averted her gaze to the beautifully carved ceiling, to the bedposts, to the fireplace in the far side of the bedchamber. Anywhere but upon her husband, for she could feel the embarrassment vibrating off of him as his inability to insert himself into her stretched on and on.
Eventually, as the onlookers grew uncomfortable and the silence grew deafening, king Henry had rolled off her and stormed out of the room without a word.
Every night since then, Henry had entered her bedchamber with a sour look on his face. He had disrobed without uttering a single word to her and jerked his head in the direction of the bed, indicating to her that she was to lay down in it.
But every night, he continued unable to perform.

"You mean I should…touch him?" Anne said then, looking from one lady to another, "Down there?"
The young Kathryn Howard shrugged, a sad expression crossing her face briefly, "Men enjoy the touch of a woman," she explained, and the twenty-four-year-old queen wondered what her fifteen-year-old lady had been made to endure for the pleasures of men at such a young age to know of such vulgarities.
But then Anne nodded her head, remembering the lust she had seen in Henry's eyes upon their very first meeting at Rochester, and at dinner that same day.
There was some passion within him for her. She had simply done something unbeknownst to her that had extinguished it. And it was now up to her to reignite it in him.

"You are right, Kathryn," the queen eventually said, "I shall do what I must to revive his liking of me. I only wish I knew what I had done to cause such sudden distaste from him. So that I might know never to do it again."

Later that night, Queen Anne had been prepared for her husband's entrance into her chambers at the usual hour.
But this night she had already dismissed her ladies, and upon his arrival, Anne instantly let her robe fall from her slender shoulders onto a pile at her feet.
She stood stark naked by the bed, with nothing but the shadows of the dimly lit room covering parts of her bare body. But the parts she knew he would most like, were clear to see.
She held his gaze intently, aware that he was trying hard not to break eye contact to ogle her firm breasts and her flat belly.
But then he could no longer control himself, and his hungry eyes roamed over the plains of her curves. Anne forced herself not to cover her intimate areas with her hands subconsciously, for she knew that her body was his to behold.
Despite what Anne knew had happened to his previous wives, she wanted him to want her.
So much hung in the balance for her and her family, and she wished for nothing more than to make her family proud. To be the one to join her Protestant house with that of the great country of England.
But despite all that, Anne had also wanted to have her husband look upon her as he had done on that first day, when he had ridden to her in disguise and his eyes had shone with joy to see her standing by the window.
When he had kissed her hand and she had seen all his worries melt away.
Well…he was certainly looking now.

Henry walked towards her hastily then, unable to contain his need of her, and as he reached her, he crushed his mouth over hers, his big hands grabbing her buttocks urgently.

Anne suddenly felt a warmth of pride coursing through her.

She had achieved what she had hoped to – for her husband to feel an urge for her, and to want to consummate their lawful marriage.

With a groan, he let go of her and ripped his own robe off of him, and their naked bodies pressed up against each other's.

A putrid smell wafted up then, to which Anne stiffened slightly. But Henry did not notice – thank God – for she knew that his ulcerous leg was a cause of great embarrassment to her ageing husband.

But she pushed her disgust aside as he continued to kiss her greedily.

His tongue was suddenly in her mouth – something she had not been prepared for – and she pulled away slightly before quickly allowing him to continue.

A wife must give herself to her husband, her mother's voice reminded her inside her head, *whatever he may wish to do, you allow him.*

At the thought, her body relaxed. She was doing her duty.

And tonight, Anne would do anything she had to, to finalise this wedded union.

Slowly, she pressed her hands onto his large, hairy chest. Then she slid one hand down the length of his torso and between them. She found his erect manhood triumphantly and grabbed it, a pleased smile tugging at her lips as he continued to kiss her eagerly.

At her touch, Henry moaned.

Then, in one swift motion, he spun her around and bent her over the mattress of her four-poster bed.

She gasped in shock at the sudden action, but she allowed him to take the lead since she was inexperienced in all manner of marital passions.

He pushed himself inside her forcefully then with one great groan, and Anne – who had been unprepared for such brutality – cried out in pain and she felt as though she was being torn apart.

Henry ignored her scream and instead he grabbed her hips forcibly and rammed himself inside her again and again.

Each time Anne called out in agony, her throat becoming raw from the shouts.

But after just six violent pumps, Anne could take it no more.

"STOP IT!" she screamed hysterically as she rolled away from him, smacking his hands off her hips.

Henry stared bewildered at his naked wife, whom he was so close to inseminating, had she not rolled away.

Her face was red and covered in tears, her eyes bloodshot and looking up at him with such disgust that he felt his manhood deflate in that very moment.

They stared at one another for several seconds, neither of them bothering to cover their nakedness or their disappointment.

And in that moment, as the beautiful Anne of Cleves continued to bravely stare him down – robbing him of his victory, *yet again* – Henry knew that he would do anything to be rid of her. Even if it meant lying to the entire world, and to God, that this short yet passionate consummation had never happened.

June 1540

Unbeknownst to the young Prince Edward, all manner of Hell was breaking loose at his father's court at Greenwich Palace. But at the age of not yet three-years-old, Edward was not only unaware of adult troubles, but he was also firmly shielded from them. For to unsettle the boy in any way would be going against the king's orders to keep him from harm.

He was growing up to be a strong and healthy boy, cared for and entertained by several governesses and servants every hour of every day.

Through the king's insistence that the prince's residence be scrubbed to perfection twice daily, the boy had overcome the dangerous early years of life without so much as a cough, and with each year that passed, his father grew more relaxed in the knowledge that this boy would – *finally* – be his legacy.

"He is a clever and sweet-natured boy, Your Majesty," the prince's governess, Lady Margaret Bryan, told the king one morning as she delivered the weekly news of his son.

"I have never known a child to be so full of pretty tricks," she concluded, a smile wrinkling her weathered face.

The king nodded agreeably then, expressing joy for the first time since the Lady Bryan's entrance into the great hall.

"Excellent news," he said, "I shall begin considering tutors for the boy soon to make sure he follows well in his father's footsteps as a great king."

Lady Bryan noticed that the king cast a sideways glance at the queen beside him as he spoke, no doubt conveying a snub at her for failing him in the marriage bed.

She looked briefly at the pale-faced queen who sat rigidly beside her husband, and the Lady Bryan wondered if they continued unable to consummate their marriage.

It was the talk of the entire country – king Henry's inability to become sufficiently aroused by his wife to conclude their wedded union.

But the Lady Bryan – like every other courtier who had lain eyes upon the German princess – could not understand his dislike of her.

Since altering her fashion to that of the English traditions, the queen's beauty had been enhanced even more so than when she first arrived in England. She was slender, with a slim waist and a long torso. Her skin was clear and her forehead high. Her eyes were a magnificent shade of green, surrounded by light coloured, yet long, eyelashes.

Her nose was a little large, and her face a little round. But the Lady Bryan could not possibly believe that those minor flaws – if one could even call them that – were responsible for the king's…impotence.

No, she mustn't think that way.

Of course, it must be the queen's fault.

For the king was…well, the *king*. He was next to God.

And his precious son – as well as his daughters – were proof enough that he was strong and capable.

For a reason unknown to the rest of the country, the gentle queen beside him must have done something to render him unwilling. And if it wasn't her looks, then she must have done something to greatly offend her lord husband.

For of course, a wife would always be to blame for her husband's shortcomings.

July 1540

Six months after the elaborate union to cement England's alliance with the Protestant House of Cleves, King Henry announced that his marriage to Anne of Cleves was to be annulled.

"She is not my true wife!" he bellowed at his Secretary of State, Thomas Cromwell, who had suggested and arranged the marriage, "She was pre-contracted to marry the Duke of Lorraine's son. Her unsatisfactory looks aside, she was never mine to wed, and I now believe that my inability to consummate the marriage was God's way of showing me that I would have been with another man's wife!"

Thomas Cromwell, who had pushed for this alliance in order to strengthen the Protestant cause within England, was receiving the brunt of the king's anger now that he was desperate for a way out of his latest marriage.

The Imperial-French alliance which had initially awakened the King of England's fear of a Catholic foreign invasion, had recently crumbled, France and Spain being – yet again – at each other's throats and therefore no immediate threat to England.

And with this alliance ended before it had truly begun, Henry no longer saw the need to shackle himself to a wife he did not care for, simply to guarantee the safety her noble family had offered.

"See to it that I am free of that…that Flander's Mare before too long," the king ordered his former favourite councillor, "I have my eye on a lady who has reawakened my desire to fornicate. Yet more proof that it was the Cleves wench who is to blame for this failure."

Chapter 6

1541
Greenwich Palace, London

Prince Edward – the light of his father's life and the future of England – was struck down with fever at the tender age of four-years-old.

"What has caused it?" the king asked, his voice breaking with concern.

"We do not know, Your Majesty," replied Sir William Sydney, who had been appointed to run the prince's household upon his birth.

"Have you not been cleaning the household as I had instructed, Sydney?!" the king bellowed then, hoping to find someone to blame for this most disturbing news.

Sir William Sydney flinched at the king's loud voice.

"We have been scrubbing the walls and floors twice daily, as Your Majesty had ordered," Sydney stammered, "The prince's illness cannot be blamed on lack of cleanliness."

The king rubbed his hands over his face before grabbing his new wife's delicate hand and crushing it in his.

Henry VIII's newest wife, Kathryn Howard, was the former lady-in-waiting to his previous wife, Anne of Cleves.

And though she was no more than fifteen-years-old, Kathryn Howard was entirely aware not to react to her husband's painful grip of her hand. She frowned in discomfort instead, but she did not utter a word, conscious that the king was in desperate need of a lifeline in the face of the worst news imaginable – the potential death of his son and heir.

"I will dispatch my own personal physician to him," the king said then after a moment of silence, "Doctor William Butts will surely know how to save my precious boy!" he said, before turning to look at the teenaged queen beside him.

"And you!" he spat at her, "See to it that you conceive soon! Isn't that what you're here for?!"

Richmond Palace, Surrey

Shortly after the king's physician had arrived at Richmond Palace and examined the pale-faced, shivering young prince, he sent word back to his master that the boy would likely not live past the night.
Henry saddled his horse right away and, followed by his king's guards, he raced to his son's bedside without a single care for his own safety.
Upon entering the prince's chambers, Henry froze.
Henry's most precious child lay motionless and ashen underneath many blankets of wool on his four-poster bed.
He looked tiny in the middle of that great mattress.
His golden hair was matted with sweat as it clung to the child's forehead. The only proof that he was alive at all was the unsettled movement of his closed eyes as he slept.

"It is quartan fever, Your Majesty," the king's physician mumbled as Henry took a step towards his son.
The king nodded his balding head but did not reply.
Instead, he sank down to his knees at the foot of the great bed, clasped his big hands together tightly and prayed to the good Lord above to save his favourite child.

God had listened.
After ten days of lethargy and very little ability to do much more than sit up to sip his warm broth, Prince Edward awoke from his feverish slumber with a smile on his face and a spring in his step.

"It's a miracle," Henry had marvelled as he looked upon his son's rosy cheeks and shining grey eyes, so much like his mother's.

A pang of guilt pierced through Henry then as he continued to watch his son be fawned over by his governess and servants, and he wondered if this had been some form of punishment from God for being rid of two more wives since his son's birth. He could not be sure, but the king said a silent prayer nonetheless, thanking Him for his benevolence, and Henry whispered a promise that his current wife, the beautiful and young Kathryn Howard, would certainly be his last.

But of course, Henry VIII would not be made to stay with a wife who failed to conceive after eighteen long months of marriage.

After all, Jane Seymour had taken seven months to conceive, and she had brought nothing more to the marriage than her *potential* to conceive sons, as her mother had done for her husband.

But Kathryn Howard had had youth and beauty on her side, which had been an invaluable reason to give her more time than Jane. And *still* she failed to do the only thing she was meant to do!

"Goddamn women," Henry mumbled as he considered his bad luck with the weaker sex. And he wondered just how he might be rid of his latest failure when he *just* proclaimed her to be 'his rose without a torn' to all of England.

Henry rubbed a hand over his forehead when there was a sudden knock at the door.

The king called for them to enter but he remained seated by the roaring fire in his bedchamber.

"Archbishop Cranmer," Henry said in greeting, his grey eyebrows furrowed in confusion for the unannounced visit at this late hour.

Cranmer stepped inside and bowed to the king, then he turned slightly and held out his hand, to which one of the young queen's ladies emerged from the doorway behind the archbishop.

Henry waved his hand in the air and shook his head, "I am not in the mood for that tonight, Cranmer," he said.

The young lady looked from the king to Cranmer with wide eyes, and Henry couldn't help but think she looked as dumb as she looked ugly.

What was Cranmer thinking bringing such an ugly wench to him when he could choose to bed any lady he wanted –

"No, my liege," Cranmer said, breaking the king's rambling thoughts, "This is Joan Bulmer."

The king frowned, showing his continued confusion.

Cranmer cleared his throat and took a step towards Henry.

"The lady Bulmer brings grave news about Her Majesty," Cranmer explained, "News…which Your Majesty will like to hear given your recent…disinterest in the queen."

Henry looked over Cranmer's shoulder at the stumpy girl behind him, "Come," he said as he waved her closer, "What news do you bring that I might find of value."

Joan approached the king with a great smile on her face, "Your Majesty," she said breathlessly, as though she were about to share a piece of gossip with her similarly dim-witted friends, "I bring news of the queen's…close friendship…with your groom."

Henry frowned, "Culpepper?"

Joan nodded, her face half in darkness as she stood by the fire, "Yes, that one," she said with a sly grin, "A Mr. Thomas Culpepper."

February 1542

Despite the lack of evidence that would see queen Kathryn Howard found guilty of adultery, the King of England put forth a bill of attainder that declared it treason for a queen consort to fail to disclose her sexual history to the king within twenty days of their marriage.

Though Kathryn and Henry had already been married eighteen months…

It was with this bill that the seventeen-year-old queen was sentenced to death, regardless as to whether she had in fact committed adultery or not, since she had – of course – failed to disclose her past sexual relationships within the allotted time frame.

And it was Henry's way of making it clear to the world that, in one way or another, Kathryn Howard was a whore.

The former queen was kept imprisoned without a formal trial to await her untimely death. And as her final royal wish she requested that the block be brought up to her cell, so that she may practice how to lay her head upon it in her final moment.

Kathryn, though she had been born and raised of low birth, remained graceful and regal on the morning of the 13th of February, and she went to the scaffold as composed as any queen could be as she faced her death.

She was then blindfolded as she mumbled for God to have mercy on her soul, and she knelt down slowly, feeling for the block before her with trembling hands.

Then, just as she had practiced for many hours the night before, she lay her head down gracefully onto the block, and uncomplainingly awaited the swift blow of the axe.

October 1543

At the age of six-years-old, a prince was henceforth considered to be on the path to becoming an adult.

Infantile things were from this moment a thing of the past, and as a result, following Prince Edward's birthday, king Henry ordered for the prince's chambers be completely remodelled, removing all manner of childishness, and to mirror the king's own.

It was the very beginning of Henry's desire of shaping his son into one day becoming the very image of himself, and to follow in his footsteps as one of the greatest kings England had ever known.

Flemish tapestries were hung throughout the boy's apartments, depicting the same Biblical scenes that the king, his father, favoured.

But it did not stop there, for as well as duplicating the king's own chambers, the prince had also received an entirely new wardrobe, filled with miniature versions of his father's own gold-stitched shirts, velvet hose and jackets and ermine trimmed furs.

The prince was – quite literally – being shaped into the very image of his father.

But the change that was most significant to the young prince, was the sudden dismissal of all his female attendants. Including the lady who had practically raised him from birth, the Lady Margaret Bryan.

But the prince knew better than to demonstrate his upset. He was the son of the king! A man in the making! And men did not snivel like little girls.

In the Lady's stead, Prince Edward was appointed two new tutors who would begin his formal teachings of what it meant to rule England one day.

Richard Cox and John Cheke were highly respected scholars whom the king himself had chosen for his son's education.

"I want the boy's education to follow humanist lines, of course," the king told the prince's two new tutors, "But ensure there is an emphasis on Latin, Greek, grammar and oration."

The two elderly men bowed their heads at their king.

"However," the king continued, "He should also be taught fencing and riding of course! As well as music and all manner of courtly pursuits. My boy shall be as well-rounded as his father, in all manner of things."

Richard Cox smiled faintly then, noting the underlying double meaning of the king's words, his rotund stature having become undeniable of late. Yet it seemed it had not been the king's intention to point out his expanding body, and so Richard quickly disguised his smile as a cough.

The king continued.

"I want to be clear that Prince Edward is to receive a religious education that is broadly Evangelical," he said, "After all, is it *crucial* that my heir should respect and promote the royal supremacy over that of the Church. I shall also entrust Archbishop Cranmer to visit the prince regularly, to instil in him the righteousness of our reforms."

"Of course, Your Majesty," John Cheke replied with a nod of his balding head, "There will be no place for religious conservatives in the prince's schoolroom."

The king nodded at that before waving his big hand to dismiss them.

"You are to be betrothed to the infant Queen of Scotland, Your Grace," archbishop Cranmer said on one of his weekly visits to the prince.

"Betrothed?" said the young, blond-haired prince, his light eyebrows furrowing together in innocent naivety.

"To be married," Cranmer explained before pulling a letter from his sleeve. He smiled reassuringly at the young boy and then dropped his gaze to the paper in his hands, "It says it is your noble father's greatest wish that you and the young Queen Mary be wed, to unify the two countries of England and Scotland, and to put an end to the age-old enmity between them."

Edward nodded slowly, "Then I shall wed her," he said with certainty, "If it is my father's wish."

Cranmer folded the paper in half and looked upon his prince, "Your father is the greatest king to ever have lived," he said, "You do well in accepting his divine wish, for he knows God's will."

The prince inhaled deeply then, his chest aching with pride for his father, and gratitude that God had chosen *him* to follow in his footsteps.

And yet a strange, heavy feeling began to form in the pit of the young boy's stomach. But he inhaled deeply to settle himself, brushing it off as excitement.

For all that mattered was that Edward do *exactly* what his great father wished of him, and in turn, Edward would be following his father's path towards greatness.

April 1544

Although the lords in Scotland had initially agreed to the match of the young Prince Edward to their even younger Queen Mary, six months later they simply changed their minds.

"My father is seething at the news," Prince Edward told his best – and only – friend, Barnaby Fitzpatrick as they sat opposite each other at a chess table, their heads almost touching as Edward conveyed the secret information to his confidant.

"And you are not?" his friend asked.

Barnaby had been sent from Ireland by his father years ago, as a pledge of loyalty to king Henry when his father gave up his claim to the kingdom of Ossory as a part of the surrender of Ireland.

He was two years older than his prince and had been granted a courtly education when he had befriended Edward some months ago, upon their first meeting at a Christmastide at court, when Edward had been called upon to attend the Christmas festivities to meet the new queen Catherine Parr.

And before long, Barnaby and Edward had become inseparable. So much so that the king had granted he be transferred to the prince's household and to continue his education with the king's son himself.

It had been a tremendous honour to his family. And Barnaby had thanked the good Lord above for his incredibly good fortune.

Edward shrugged in response to his friend's question then.

"I shall do my duty," he said, "With whoever I shall one day marry."

Barnaby nodded as he continued to examine the chess board before him, disinterested in the adult topic of politics and marital union. Then he swiftly reached over and moved his black-squared bishop.

"Checkmate!" Barnaby whispered victoriously, a lopsided grin spreading across his face as he met Edward's narrowed eyes.

"You're supposed to let me win!" Edward whined then as he reached across the table, attempting to pry his king from Barnaby's closed fist.

"No chance, Your Grace!" Barnaby laughed, "You'll have to do better than that!"

*

Though King Henry referred to his son as the realm's most precious jewel, he never actually spent any time with him, leaving Edward to, quite frankly, grow up without a mother *or* a father.

But the king showed his affection in other ways, gifting the boy all the best things money could buy, including having his study books be covered in gold and set with rubies, diamonds, and sapphires.

Prince Edward never wanted for anything…as long as it was material.

Though at the age of six Edward was henceforth considered an adult, his child's mind struggled to understand why he felt so utterly lonely all the time, though he was constantly surrounded by people.

His father claimed to love him above all others, yet he never visited.

His uncles were fighting in Scotland in retaliation to his failed betrothal to their Scottish Queen. Although they had never shown much of an interest in him anyway.

His beloved sister Mary was suffering from her usual bought of illness more often lately. His other sister, secluded in Hertfordshire.

His mother was dead and buried because of him.

And so, it seemed the only person Edward could really turn to in times of sorrow was his friend Barnaby.

Edward was grateful to have a friend such as he, someone who did not constantly pamper his every whim and who actually treated him like a real person, rather than a precious object.

Though I do loathe to lose at chess against him, Edward thought.

But he was glad to have Barnaby within his household to run wild, and to get up to mischief with.

For it was moments spent with Barnaby that made his dull days seem brighter. Even when the activities of the days were all the same; if Barnaby was with him, Edward felt a warmth inside him that he hoped would never turn cold.

May 1544

"The king and his parliament have passed a new Act of Succession," Archbishop Cranmer told the young Prince and his household one afternoon.
Edward looked up from his journal, "What of it?" he said, to which the archbishop noted – not for the first time – how much more mature his wordings sounded to that of a six-year-old.
Cranmer took a seat opposite the young boy, "It states that after Your Grace, your sister Mary is to succeed you, should you die without heirs."
Edward put down the quill he had been writing with and narrowed his eyes.
"Should I die without heirs," he repeated.
It was not a question, but Cranmer replied nonetheless, feeding the boy the fatherly attention he knew the young prince craved.
"Precisely," was all Cranmer said, knowing it would be enough to further the conversation.
Edward cocked his head to one side then, "Am I to assume my lord father is unlikely to have any more sons by queen Catherine?"
Cranmer smiled, "She has not yet conceived and is not likely to, no. This being her third marriage without a single conception would suggest the lady is fruitless."
Edward frowned deeply, knowing of his father's bad luck in finding a worthy wife since his mother's death.
"Surely my father ought to be rid of her then?!" he said angrily, a knot of unease constricting his stomach suddenly.

Stupid woman!
Edward couldn't help the thought from popping in his head. He loved his stepmother and believed her to be a noble lady.
But how dare she fail his father so!
But then, it seemed women had always managed to fail the men in their lives, and Edward was beginning to understand that they really *were* the weaker sex.
Noticing the prince's anger growing, Cranmer waved his hand in the air, taking this opportunity of the prince's distress to his advantage.

"Do not trouble yourself with the failings of lesser women, Your Grace," he said, "The king is strong. He may yet draw up another Act if the queen produces a son."
At that, Edward's shoulders relaxed slightly.

"But always remember, my dearest son in Christ," Cranmer continued as he leaned a little closer to the prince then, "When the time comes for Your Grace to rule England, I shall be by your side to guide you."
Cranmer offered Edward a comforting smile, which the boy returned gratefully.

August 1545

Court had become a dangerous place to be when the King of England had declared war not only on France but also on Scotland the year before, leading to a long-winded war on both countries, and to a disastrous defeat at Acrumn, Scotland.
The invasion of France had begun well enough however, English troops having managed to siege the city of Boulogne almost immediately, adding it to England's growing territory in France along with Calais, which had been captured by Edward III in 1347.

But the victory did not extend any further when England's ally in the war against France – Spain – had turned on England and made their own peace treaty with the French, leaving England with no other choice but to retreat; the war concluded as practically futile.

"It is of course the Duke of Suffolk's fault!" the young prince bellowed as he received news of England's failed siege, his anger boiling over instantly and uncontrollably.

"The moment my most glorious father left Boulogne under Charles Brandon's defence, he lost it!"

"The outcome of war is like that of the toss of a coin," Edward's tutor, John Cheke, told him as he waved the messenger away and continued to calmly peruse the Greek textbook before him, "Return your mind to your studies, Your Grace, and you may yet learn how to avoid such mistakes as what has brought on your father's defeat."

The insinuation that his father was in any way to blame for this latest loss for England, angered the prince immensely.

"My father's defeat?!" Edward repeated, his voice raised and his grey eyes blazing, "Have you understood nothing of the report!? The war was lost when my father returned to England. He left the finalities of his *victory* to his most trusted men. And it is *they* who have squandered their chance at triumph!"

He was on his feet now, his temper having shot him off his seat, and still he could not control the rage he was feeling in his chest. As the prince glowered at his tutor menacingly, John Cheke looked up at his ward with a bored expression on his face, his hands clasped together lazily over his belly as he sat back and waited for yet another of the prince's tantrum to deflate.

He was used to Edward's outbursts – so much like his father's. But it wasn't his job to berate the prince or to educate his character. That had not been discussed when the king specified his son's strict education on politics and religion.

"My father is the greatest king to have ever lived!" the red-faced prince continued, "And for you to suggest that *you* shall ever teach me to be better than he...you are mistaken! For I alone can do that! I alone can strive to achieve greatness beyond my father's successes by firstly making sure I follow in his glorious footsteps! Do not presume to know how to rule better than the great King Henry VIII himself and his most princely son and heir!"

When the boy had ceased to spout his superiority, Cheke raised his brows and sat up to resume his reading. But when the prince did not return to his seat, Cheke raised his head to meet the boy's stare.

"Was there anything else, Your Grace?" Cheke asked casually, as if he had not just now been berated by a self-important seven-year-old.

September 1545

Prince Edward and Archbishop Cranmer's relationship had developed quickly due to his weekly visits since the boy's sixth birthday nearly two years prior.

It had almost been pitiful, the archbishop thought, how desperate the young boy had been for even a scrap of attention and praise from someone other than his tutors.

And soon, Cranmer noticed that the prince had begun hanging off of his every word.

Before long, Edward and he were in regular communication in between his visits, the prince going so far as to correspond with his royal father through letters he would send the archbishop.

In fact, Cranmer had been so successful in nurturing the young and impressionable Tudor heir, that Edward soon came to look upon the Protestant archbishop as a fatherly figure.

"A letter, your excellency," a messenger's voice called then, pulling Cranmer from his thoughts as he stood by the open window of his chambers.

"Ah," the archbishop muttered as he took the folded note from the young man and waved him away.

This would be the prince's response to Cranmer's seemingly innocent letter sent the previous evening, enquiring over Edward's wellbeing.

But of course, Cranmer's correspondence with Edward had never been innocent, even the simplest of messages being laden with underlying, ulterior motives to communicate with the young prince at all.

And each note sent, would be yet another carving made towards Cranmer building his perfect, dancing puppet.

The archbishop unfolded the prince's letter.

I am not unmindful of the kindness you bestow onto me, and I hope that you may live many years, and continue to be my honoured father by your godly and wholesome advice.

Cranmer read the short note with a sly smile beneath his bearded face, and he shook his head in delighted disbelief at how easy it had been to infiltrate the mind of a lonely little prince.

My honoured father, Cranmer re-read, then breathed a laugh.

He sat down at his writing desk then before slowly dipping his quill into the inkpot to write his reply.

The words flowed easily onto the paper, his words of praise and adoration not being entirely untrue. Yet it relieved Cranmer to know that it seemed Prince Edward would most likely continue to pursue his father's path to reform the country.

And he hoped that, with his continued drip-feeding of strong Protestant beliefs, Edward would take England that one step further than his ambiguous father had ever done.

Chapter 7

25th January 1547
Westminster, London

  Two years later, at the age of fifty-five, king Henry VIII had been struck down with what would be his final illness.
Throughout the month of January, Henry had remained secluded within his chambers at Westminster, where he had retreated to when he had begun to feel the onset of weakness.
He had hoped to recover, of course. But it seemed this last bought of lethargy would be his end.
He had no more energy left in him now. Not since his dearest friend, Charles Brandon had died shortly after their failure at Boulogne in France.
Henry had buried five wives.
He had fathered dozens of children, legitimate as well as bastards. Alive, as well as dead.
And now he only had three remaining children to survive him.
He had managed to produce one son, at least.
Though it had taken nearly twenty-six years of failures to achieve his goal…
And now he was leaving this world, but the boy was not yet ready. Edward was not old enough to rule without a Council of Regency to advise him.
Henry knew he had to unite the different factions that would be jostling for power in these his final days.
For one man alone to be in complete charge of his heir must not come to pass. A Lord Protector would be absolutely out of the question.
There *must* be a balanced council to support the young boy in his kingly duties.

27th January 1547

Unfortunately, King Henry's epiphany had come too late, and his pleas for unity were ignored once those around him had realised that their king was slipping in and out of consciousness more often with each passing day.
And they all set about on their own paths in search for ultimate power.
"Go fetch..." the king wheezed during one of his short moments of wakefulness, "...archbishop Cranmer."
Henry knew his time was nearing, and he had to make sure he would die a Christian death.
Upon Cranmer's arrival at Westminster however, the old king had slipped back into unconsciousness and showed very little sign of life at all.
Cranmer looked from the morbidly obese king laying ashen-faced on the royal bed, to the king's councilmen, but they only shrugged in response.
No one knew how to approach the subject of death to Henry VIII.
It had been a sensitive topic for the king in the last decade, to say the least. To predict or to suggest the monarch's death had even been declared as high treason by the king.
And so, none of his council had yet been brave enough to tell Henry that he was, in fact, dying.
Archbishop Cranmer sighed heavily then, "I shall do it," he told the cowardly councillors, before taking a step towards the king.

Cranmer leaned over the dying king and whispered to him that he must offer up his confession and receive his Last Rites in order to die a Christian death.
But the king did not respond. And a cold sweat broke out between Cranmer's shoulder blades.

Cranmer took Henry's fat hand in his. He could not allow the king to die without at least acknowledging God's mercy.
How ironic it would be if King Henry VIII of England would have such an ending…

"Your Majesty must *at least* squeeze my hand as a sign that you put your trust in God," Cranmer whispered hoarsely into Henry's cold and clammy ear.
He stared at the dying king, willing him to squeeze his hand in acknowledgment.
But he did not.
Cranmer lay Henry's hand down gently after a moment.
He knew what he had to do…
And so, instead of turning a worried face to the councillors, he nodded his head slowly, as though in response to something the king had said.
When in actuality, he hadn't uttered a single word; much less acknowledged that Cranmer was even there.
But the archbishop would not allow the great Henry VIII – who had risen him from nothing and had made him one of the most powerful men in England – to be remembered as having died without God's blessing.
He *had to* maintain this stately façade…

"The king squeezed my hand firmly," he lied to the advisors then, who remained at the threshold of the king's chambers.
And as though Henry had awaited Cranmer's false statement, the fat king let out one last long sigh.
Then a wet gurgle.
Followed by a choking sound. And finally, a phlegmy splutter.
Then there was silence.

31st January 1547

Henry VIII's death was kept a secret for three whole days.

Three days in which his councilmen scrambled about, falsifying documents with the king's seal.

But he had already been dead.

However, nobody but those surrounding him had known of his actual date of death. And they took complete advantage of the people's lack of knowledge, going so far as to request servants to bring food to the king's chambers in order to continue on the charade that he was still clinging onto life, until those seeking power had succeeded in their game.

The king's final wish that his nine-year-old son be supported in his ruling by a Council of Regency – a large group of especially selected advisors, rather than one man alone – had been destroyed and rewritten by none other than Edward Seymour, the late queen, Jane Seymour's, brother.

Seymour's reputation for military efficiency during the wars in Scotland and France, as well as the fact that he was the new king's own uncle, gained him the support he needed to attain the other councilmember's consent.

And upon the old king's death, Edward Seymour appointed himself as the new king's Lord Protector, to rule in the boy's stead, until he came of age.

Much to the displeasure and envy of the new king's other uncle, Thomas Seymour.

Hertford Castle

It was a day like any other, filled with endless studying of language and politics, practicing of horse riding and perfecting of oration.

It was a day like any other, a swift game of cards or backgammon in between lessons with Barnaby, hidden in the shadows to avoid detection from their tutors.

It was a day like any other, being dragged back to the classroom, being made to dissect another document in Latin, Greek, or French.

It was a day like any other...

Until it wasn't.

"Your father is dead, Your Grace," Edward Seymour, Earl of Hertford, told his nephew, "You are England's new king."

At the words, Edward's face drained of colour, and yet his uncle noticed that his back straightened, as though Edward were trying to add a couple of inches to his height.

In an effort to appear more grown up? More kingly?

It didn't matter, Edward Seymour thought, *For he shall not actually rule for years to come.*

Before the boy had had a chance to respond, Edward Seymour grabbed him by the shoulder, steering him out of the hall and through the castle gates.

"Come," he said, "We must go to Enfield in Middlesex. To keep you safe."

The new king shrugged his shoulder free of his uncle's grasp, a deep frown etched between his brows as he stared up at this man claiming to be his uncle but never once having bothered to even get to know him.

"Get your hand off me, Sir!" he shouted, "How dare you lay a hand on your king!"

Edward Seymour had stared back, bewildered at the boy's temper.

He certainly is his father's son, he had thought.

The Earl of Hertford knew that, in order to maintain power, it was crucial that he retain custody of the young king.

And so it seemed that for the boy to come willingly, he would need to take a less obvious approach.

The boy king watched as his uncle crouched down before him then, so that he was at eye level with him.

"We must make sure to keep you hidden for a short while, Your Majesty," he said, his eyes shining with fear, "In case a European country were to use this moment of weakness within England to wage war."

Young Edward's blond eyebrows shot up, "War?" he repeated, his shoulder's dropping slightly as his anger was replaced with worry.

His uncle nodded before straightening up, "We must move you to a more secure location," he said, "And order for all ports and roads into London to be closed."

The boy's gasp caught in his throat, and in that moment, he realised his naivety. For he had not even considered the possibility of war.

"Before his death," Edward Seymour continued as he turned and walked towards the horses saddled outside, fully aware that the boy would now follow, fear having swayed him into submission, "your father appointed me your Lord Protector," he lied.

"Lord Protector?" Edward echoed as he watched his uncle swing onto his horse effortlessly.

"I shall help you rule England until you are of age, Your Majesty," Seymour explained.

Two servants aided the boy into his smaller horse's saddle.

"To advise you in matters of state that you, as a young man, would not be knowledgeable in."

Edward felt a pinch of resentment at his uncle's choice of words.

But he nodded his head nonetheless, since this very conversation had proven just that – that though Edward was born to Henry VIII, born to rule, born to be a king, he did not have the first clue how to *actually* manage an entire kingdom.

20th February 1547
Westminster, London

Four days after Henry VIII's embalmed body had been interred in Jane Seymour's tomb as per his wishes, his only surviving son was crowned as the new King of England.
At nine o'clock in the morning the young King Edward VI, accompanied by his uncle, the new Lord Protector, was escorted by barge to Whitehall.
There he was conducted to the Court of Augmentations which was hung richly with cloth of arras and cloth of estate.
Edward wore a cloak of crimson velvet with a long train, trimmed with ermine furs throughout. His gloves were garnished with ribbons of gold and the cap on his head was of a rich black velvet.
The little king then processed to Westminster Abbey for the coronation ceremony, a long parade ahead of him.
He walked slowly under a canopy carried by four Knights of the Garter, while his Lord Protector walked ahead of him carrying St Edward's crown.
Behind King Edward were members of his council, John Dudley, William Parr, and his other uncle Thomas Seymour, who all bore his heavy train.
They were surrounded by onlookers who waved and cheered, mesmerized as they observed the grand occasion from behind the barriers decorated with flowers.
Upon entering the abbey, Edward spotted the great throne at the end of the vast cloister. His heart began to suddenly hammer against his chest at the sight of it, and at the memory of who had sat upon it before him.
His majestic and glorious father. The most noble king England had ever known.

And now he, the little boy king, would – quite literally – be taking his place. And it was a big throne to fill.

Edward swallowed hard, pushing his anxiety down into the deepest pits of his stomach, hoping to display an aura not of childish fear, but of mature tranquillity.

As he approached the throne, however, Edward was appalled to see not one – as was custom during a long and arduous coronation – but *two* cushions placed upon the seat on top of one another.

One of black velvet embroidered with gold. The other of cloth of tissue… and Edward was painfully aware that it had been placed there to help raise him higher.

He sat down upon them uncomplainingly, nonetheless.

Though it had been tradition since 1375 for a coronation to last twelve hours, it had been adapted by Edward's council to be no more than seven hours, in order to accommodate the young boy during this monumental and exhausting experience.

Archbishop Thomas Cranmer had also altered the coronation oath, declaring the king as supreme lawmaker – since Edward VI would be the very first monarch to ever be crowned as a Protestant king and under the Protestant Church of England.

Edward was anointed with the holy oil.

He was then crowned with not one, but three separate crowns; each being placed upon his head individually and trumpets sounding in between each crowning.

St Edward's crown came first, followed by the imperial crown, and the crowning was then finalised with a lighter, custom-made crown for the young boy's comfort during the remaining hours of the coronation.

The choir sang Te Deum as a ring of gold was placed on the new king's wedding finger, and he was carefully handed St Edward's staff in one hand and the orb of gold placed in the other.

Edward VI sat upon his two-cushioned throne, holding onto two of the most precious objects of England as his hands trembled at their weight.

But he knew he must not let them fall.

A bead of sweat descended his forehead as the choir continued their song for what felt like hours.

But then – by the grace of God – it was concluded, and as the nobles cheered for their new king, he gratefully handed the orb and staff back to the archbishop.

Cranmer offered Edward a reassuring smile as he took the objects from the young king, and he noticed the boy exhale slowly in a secret, thankful response.

What followed were two days of celebrations.

Magnificent banquets were held at Whitehall's great hall, as well as entertainment of jousting and dancing to commemorate this glorious occasion.

And all the while, none had known that these had been the most frightening days of the young king's life – so far.

Chapter 8

March 1547

The transition from prince to king was anything but gradual. As soon as the celebrations were concluded two days after Edward's coronation, he was thrown into the deep end, and no amount of tutoring could have prepared him for what it really meant to be king.

"Despite your father's break from Rome," the Lord Protector said as he sat beside the new king at the council table, "residual elements of Catholic worship still exist."

Edward's upper lip twitched slightly at the mention of Catholicism, which he had been taught to hate above all things.

"What do you recommend, uncle?" the king asked, hoping his Lord Protector would have some suggestions on how to deal with the problem.

"There are several items to discuss today, Your Majesty," Seymour replied pedantically as he waved about the document in his hand.

The country's political, economic, military, and religious issues aside, there were social issues within his own court and council that Edward could see he had yet to master if he wished to be taken seriously.

King Edward cleared his throat, embarrassed to have spoken erroneously, "Continue."

"Another matter that needs Your Majesty's urgent attention," Seymour resumed, "is the Scots' persistent unwillingness to establish peace between our two countries. The Greenwich Peace Treaty which was signed in 1543 is yet to be implemented, and with it, your marriage to their young Queen, Mary of Scots."

Edward's throat constricted suddenly at the mention of marriage, but he knew better than to speak out of turn again.

He looked up at his uncle and then at the advisors surrounding him. None of them were even looking at him, their king, their eyes fixed instead at the Lord Protector beside him.

All except for his other uncle, Thomas Seymour, who was smiling reassuringly at young Edward.

Edward nodded at him in gratitude for his attention, then returned his gaze to his Lord Protector beside him.

"We must settle this on the battlefield," Seymour said then as he looked up and folded the paper in half.

The many men around the table nodded their heads, some mumbling "Hear, hear," in agreement.

But this time Edward could not keep from interjecting, "Surely to wage war to incite peace is somewhat ludicrous, my lord?" he said.

The men before him sniggered in response, some shaking their heads at the young boy's innocence – though his logic was of course precise.

"An excellent point, Your Majesty," Thomas Seymour said once the quiet laughter had died down, making sure to maintain a fixed eye contact with the uncertain king.

Edward smiled in appreciation for his uncle Thomas' public agreement.

But the Lord Protector cleared his throat and frowned. He knew exactly what game his brother, Thomas, was playing by trying to gain favour with the young king, no matter how shallow it may be.

Torn between displaying his annoyance at his brother and amusement at his king's naïve statement, he chose to ignore his brother's futile attempts at creating a rapport with their nephew.

"My king," Edward Seymour replied finally, an amused smile beneath his chestnut beard, "War is how we will get the Scots to submit."

April 1547

Feeling snubbed by his older brother's rise to supreme power as Lord Protector, Thomas Seymour couldn't help but believe that he had been dealt an unfair hand.
For surely, as the young king's other uncle, Thomas too should be able to hold some power within the council while his nephew was too young to rule without a regent.
The few titles that had been lain upon him by his brother to keep Thomas quiet had not been enough to satisfy the urgent need within him to increase his worth.
And so, when it became clear that his brother, the Lord Protector, would not grant him more authority, Thomas took it upon himself to attain what he needed. And he would not rest until others bowed before him.
He began by secretly giving the young King Edward an extravagant allowance of coins, since the Lord Protector had deemed the king too young to have access to the king's treasury.
"You may have this money to spend as you please," the king's uncle Thomas had told him in confidence with a wink.
Edward took the money without question, glad to finally have access to coinage. A buzzing of excitement developed in the boy's stomach then as Thomas Seymour put a finger to his lips before walking away, the pleasant weight of their secret practically burning a hole in Edward's pocket.
But Thomas' attempt to buy the king's affection had not been enough, for Edward – though he was king – had restricted ability to appoint new titles. Much less onto his uncle, whom his other uncle did not trust.

And before long, when young Edward had become accustomed to his weekly pocket money, Thomas Seymour found himself swimming in debt, and with no new titles or land to show for it. But this had not been Thomas Seymour's only ace up his sleeve.

May 1547

   Catherine Parr, now to be styled the Dowager Queen, had been honoured by her late husband, King Henry, with the permission to wear the queen's jewels until her stepson, the new king, came of age to be married.

The late king Henry had also granted her an annual income of seven-thousand pounds to support herself – enough money that, though she was no longer queen, she may continue to live as one.

Henry's generosity had stemmed from his profound gratitude for her as his final wife.

True, she had failed to conceive an heir during their marriage, and that had irked him extensively in life. But, despite her faults, she had proven herself a wonderful stepmother to not only his heir, but also his two bastardised daughters.

During her official time as stepmother to his three children, Catherine Parr had taken a keen interest in the two younger children's education, often reminding her late husband to send new textbooks, or to inform their tutors to focus on certain subjects she knew the young children struggled with.

It was her motherly affection for them each as individuals that had granted her her late husband's enduring gratitude.

However, though she did indeed receive the title, income, and queen's jewels shortly following king Henry's passing, she was promptly stripped of those privileges when she had spontaneously married the new king's own uncle in secret, just four months after king Henry's passing.

"What were you thinking, Thomas!?" Edward Seymour hissed at his younger brother moments after Thomas had sauntered into Greenwich Palace as though he himself had been crowned King of England upon bedding its former queen.

Thomas' smug smile remained intact, unperturbed by his brother's fury.

"You are not the only one who can make advancements for himself, brother," Thomas Seymour replied under his breath before attempting to sidestep the Lord Protector to join a group of lords in the palace's great hall.

Edward grabbed him forcefully by the arm and yanked him back in front of him, "You are a fool, Thomas!" he said, glancing briefly over his shoulder to gauge the courtiers' reactions, but they had not been paying attention to them, "The king will not take this insult lightly."

"Insult?" Thomas echoed, as though he hadn't considered such an outcome to his impulsive and unauthorised marriage.

Edward pulled a face that made it evident what he thought of Thomas' dense reply then, his eyebrows creased together, and his mouth pulled down in an expression that read, clear as crystal: *Idiot.*

Thomas narrowed his eyes at his brother's expression, "You are irked that I have outwitted you," he surmised incorrectly, "You denied me my request to marry either of king Henry's daughters when I asked some months ago. You claim all titles for yourself, *Duke of Somerset,*" he spat, then jabbed a finger at his brother's chest, "I too deserve to rise in station with *our* nephew upon the throne."

Thomas was right.

By the laws of reason, Thomas Seymour, as well as Edward Seymour, should be profiting from their young nephew's posterior sitting on the throne.

This was, after all, the highest their family had ever, and would ever, be able to reach.

And yet, Edward knew that if he gave too much to his foolish younger brother, that he would likely squander away *both* their chances of continuing to ride this wave of fortune. Edward, as Lord Protector, had already given his brother a place among the Privy Council as well as appointing him Lord High Admiral, and Baron of Sudeley. Was all that not enough?

"Get out of here before the king sees you," Edward said, shoving Thomas away, "I will smooth things over and make sure you do not get sent to the noose for this."

Thomas frowned. Was that really the punishment for his crime? He had expected a slap on the wrist. He had expected a stern letter, or at the most, a short banishment.

Thomas took a step back, his face creased as he tried to think of a response.

Gratitude? Annoyance? Disbelief?

He shook his head then, choosing the latter.

"You will do no such thing," Thomas accused, "You will continue to use my failings to your advantage, but *this* was not a failure. I have married the highest-ranking woman in all of England, and now you will no doubt do all in your power to sully this triumph."

Edward looked at his dim-witted brother with pity. Though he had been born the more handsome one of all their mother's children, Thomas lacked reason and logic.

"My dear brother, don't you understand that by marrying the highest-ranking woman in all of England you have done nothing to elevate yourself, but rather to drag her name down to your level and into the mud."

Thomas' eyebrows twitched with confusion.

"You have not married *up,*" Edward explained, "She has married *down.* With this marriage she has lost her station as Dowager Queen. She will lose the queen's jewels –"

"No…" Thomas whispered in horror.

"But," Edward continued, as though Thomas hadn't spoken, "I will endeavour for a lenient punishment, brother."

Thomas' face glowed red with anger and humiliation.

With nothing more needing to be said, Edward turned to leave.

"You'll regret denying me my fortunes!" Thomas called after him, to which Edward spun around to face him once more.

"Actually, Thomas," he said, "In this instance you should be glad your older brother holds enough power over the king to show you mercy. If it weren't for my high station within this court, you my friend, would be made a head shorter."

Then Edward Seymour walked away, ignoring the fact that the opposite of what he had said was just as true: That if he did not hold so much power, his little brother wouldn't be striving so recklessly to keep up.

September 1547

"What if I don't want Scotland to submit?" King Edward asked his best friend Barnaby one day.

He had received news that his army had arrived at the bank of the river Eske in Scotland, to wage war in an effort to bring peace, and the lack of sense in the situation continued to bewilder the young king.

They were walking lazily through the palace gardens, with no other company but their own – just the way King Edward preferred it.

"Does nobody consider that perhaps I, their king, do not wish to marry that Scottish girl?"

Edward was nearing his tenth birthday, an age which he hoped would bring with it courage, so that he may address his Lord Protector in a manner befitting the King of England. For Edward had not even wished for this war on Scotland to take place.

The war his father had waged in response to the Scots' rebuttal four years earlier had surely been enough of an attempt to get them to bend the knee to England. It had since been dubbed the 'Rough Wooing' because of how ludicrous it had been to attack a country who you wished to unify with...

"It is not only to obtain you a bride," Barnaby replied as he scratched at his neck, momentarily leaving red lines aglow on his milk-white skin, "Scotland is a Catholic country. To unite the two countries under a Protestant king would be an astounding outcome for your reign."

"For my reign or for my uncle's?" Edward replied as he kicked at a loose stone in his path.

Barnaby shrugged, "Your uncle is no doubt trying to inflate his reputation while he can. He knows that once you are of age, he will lose all his power."

"He has years yet before I may make my own decisions," Edward said, "By then I shall likely be married by proxy to that Scottish child."

Barnaby slapped his friend on the shoulder, "Come now, Edward," he said with a laugh, "You are the king! Surely there is some joy to be found in it."

Edward met his friend's green-eyed gaze, and he noticed – not for the first time – how hauntingly beautiful they were.

A soothing green, like sea foam.

His friend was right. He was the king. Too young to rule, but a king, nonetheless. And he would enjoy his life, goddammit!

Edward smirked mischievously then, so briefly Barnaby thought it might have been a trick of the light. But then Edward pressed his hands flat on his friend's chest and shoved him into the hedgerows before running off down the path.

"You'll never catch me!" the young king shouted as he raced ahead.

"Hey!" Barnaby called after him as he stepped out from the shrubbery, "That's cheating, *Your Highness!*"

But Edward only laughed and looked over his shoulder at Barnaby, growing smaller as the distance between them grew.

Barnaby brushed leaves off his shoulder and then pressed forward, running after Edward as fast as he could, both of them knowing he would easily catch up, for his legs were longer.

Edward's heart skipped a beat to see his friend racing after him, his chest growing fuzzy with excitement as he secretly awaited that delicious moment in which Barnaby would eventually catch him.

And just before the boys crashed together in a fit of laughter, Edward wondered if perhaps his aversion to the idea of marriage was less about the act itself, but rather for the fact that he would be made to marry a girl...

The Battle of Pinkie – as it had become known as – had been a failure.

Although Scotland had suffered a resounding defeat on the battlefield – which had led to the death of six-thousand of their men – the Scottish government refused to come to terms.

And during endless and pointless negotiations, their infant Queen Mary was smuggled out of the country and to France, where she would be betrothed to the young Dauphin of France, Francis.

"A unity with Scotland is now out of the question," one of the king's council, John Dudley, said as he shook his head, "The Treaty remains void if they do not wish to comply. We must look to other allies to strengthen England and its future."

The men around the table fell silent as they thought, their faces crumpled with worry, annoyance, and confusion.
They were all completely immersed in their own thoughts.
Which was why, when King Edward sat back with a great smile at the news, none of them even noticed.

November 1547

King Edward – as well as his beloved sister Mary – had been most displeased with their favourite stepmother, Catherine Parr, for not only re-marrying without the king's permission, but also for doing so within her year of mourning for their late father.
Edward had bonded greatly with Catherine during her marriage to his father, the lady always having shown him kindness and attention, which Edward had lacked considerably despite being his father's 'most precious jewel'.
But their relationship had soured when Catherine had betrayed the monarchy's authority by marrying in secret, and in the months that followed her disrespect, Edward had neither seen nor heard from his former stepmother.
It came as a welcome surprise then when – six months into her banishment – Catherine Parr published her third book, 'Lamentations of a Sinner', which promoted the Protestant faith by supporting the concept of justification by faith alone – a concept that the Catholic Church deemed as heresy.
With its publication, Edward could not stay mad at her for long. And it was with this noble act of loyalty to the Protestant faith, that King Edward decided his stepmother had been punished enough.
She would not be returned to her former glory; the loss of the Queen's Jewels and her titles could never be reversed due to her insult against the crown. But Edward acknowledged her nonetheless as stepmother once more and wrote to her warmly

that since she loved the word of God as he did, he could not help but love and admire her with his whole heart.

As he signed and sealed the letter to his openly Protestant former stepmother, Edward thought about his failed betrothal to Mary Queen of Scots, and who his council would suggest for him next. It seemed the continuation of the Protestant Tudor line was just as much a hot topic of discussion now as it had been during his father's reign.

After all, England was now a reforming nation. With many working tirelessly to support their king in his Protestant advancements for the country – Catherine Parr's book being but one of many wonderful developments.

And if Edward were to fail in procreating his own heir, all his and his father's hard work would be buried beneath the rubble of his Catholic sister's ruling, due to their father's reinstatement of her as Edward's heir.

Should I die childless.

The words echoed in his head, sending a shiver down the boy's spine.

He inhaled deeply to steady himself as he handed the letter to his messenger.

He was only ten, he thought then, to regain his composure. And healthy and strong, at that. There would be plenty of time to consider brides when the time was right.

But for now, Edward would concentrate on his true passion: Protestantism.

Everything else could wait.

Chapter 9

January 1548

It had been a year since the new King of England had been crowned, and he and his Protestant council had wasted no time in implementing new laws and legislations upon their people. Namely, on the matter of religion.
In order to lead his people towards a fully reformed, Protestant country, King Edward knew he would have to extinguish all Catholic doctrines during his reign.
He had grown up surrounded by Protestants. His tutors, archbishop Cranmer, even his favourite stepmother. All had been extremely influential in Edward's strong belief that Catholicism was defective, a ghastly religion of the past, one which would drag England and its people into darkness if it were allowed to resurface.
Protestantism was the light. It allowed all men, whether they were highborn or low, to practice their religion freely, without the Latin mumbo jumbo that Catholicism called for.
His father, Henry VIII, had done the country a great deed when he had allowed the publication of the Great Bible in 1539, the first official bible to be translated into English.
Yet, to the young boy's confusion, his father had continued to use liturgies in Latin throughout his reign, which still existed today. And though the former king had broken from Rome and the Pope, it seemed that he had had no true intention of committing himself wholly to doctrinal reform.
That would have to be rectified.

"The Royal Injections," archbishop Cranmer said, addressing Parliament and the king's council, "calls for the Epistle and Gospel at High Mass to henceforth be read in English."

Most of Parliament nodded their heads, while others – those who remained Catholic – gasped.

"Compline," Cranmer continued, "is to be sung in the Royal Chapel…in English. These are approved by our noble King Edward VI."

A loud murmur ensued as the members of Parliament grumbled amongst themselves. Cranmer glanced at the Lord Protector who sat amid the rest of the Privy Council – all but Thomas Seymour, his brother, who had been banished from court following his scandalous secret marriage to the former queen.

The Lord Protector nodded at Cranmer once, satisfied with the outcome so far, the members of Parliament mumbling amongst themselves being far more promising than an immediate outburst, which Seymour had feared.

"Furthermore," Cranmer called then once the whispers had begun to subside, "The king and his council are working tirelessly to continue on the country's journey to reform. Following the publication of the king's First Book of Homilies, there will be much change to the way we pray. And before long, Catholicism will be a thing of the past!"

Several Catholic members of Parliament shifted uncomfortably in their chairs then as they listened, all of which Cranmer noted for future reference, to make sure they would convert.

The First Book of Homilies was a pamphlet comprising of six articles containing thirty-three sermons which introduced the authorized reformed doctrines of the Church of England. These doctrines would be implemented in the Catholic doctrine's stead, the first stepping stone towards eradicating all Catholic superstitions, including the supposed ability of priests to turn wine and bread into the blood and body of Christ.

"We must make it clear to the priesthood," archbishop Cranmer said later that day as he and the king enjoyed a private dinner of roast hog, "that Catholic sermons are no longer to be allowed. It is ungodly to have the people believe that the bread and wine is any more than that. Priests are ordinary people."

Cranmer had a vision for the future. And he knew that to continue in the young king's good graces would be the key to unlocking that future.

Edward was nodding, his blond eyebrows knitted together in thought as he absentmindedly stroked his new puppy's little head as it rested upon his lap.

The Spaniel had been a New Year's gift from his uncle, Thomas Seymour, no doubt in the hope of being restored to his former glory. Edward had accepted the puppy elatedly. And yet his uncle had not been allowed to return to court.

"You are right of course, Cranmer," he said before falling silent for a moment as he chewed.

"I am thankful for all you have done for me," Edward said fondly then to the man who had been more a father to him than his own father had been, "But I fear there is more to be done."

An image of himself as a puppet-master sprung to Cranmer's mind suddenly. A dancing marionette of a blond boy with a wooden crown upon its head, attached at the hands and feet by strings to a handle, which Cranmer controlled.

The archbishop sniggered at the image, "Oh, my dear son in Christ," he said with a twinkle in his eye, "There is always more to be done."

March 1548

King Edward was sitting at the top table in the great hall as his court ate and laughed merrily before him.
Just as his father had done before him, Edward ordered for a grand banquet to take place whenever possible to show the court – and England – that the country was rich and plentiful.
All who the king held dear were invited, his stepmothers Anne of Cleves and Catherine Parr, as well as both his half-sisters, Elizabeth, and Mary. The music was loud, and the wine was flowing, many courtiers having taken to the dancefloor.
The court was cheerful as Edward had hoped, knowing that his father king Henry had placed great importance on the display of fortune and merriment.
But this day was bringing back memories for the young king. Flashes of a former life not so long ago, when he had been just a year younger in age, but a lifetime younger in responsibility.
In fact, if Edward squinted, he could almost pretend like this was the court of Henry VIII once more. And not his.
How glorious that would be.
But the newly added tables and low-sitting benches before the king distorted his image of his father's perfect court.
His sisters Mary and Elizabeth sat upon those low-sitting benches as they ate their food as elegantly as two princesses.
But, of course, they were *not* princesses. They were bastards.
His father had made that perfectly clear.
Both their mothers had been nothing more than deceitful harlots, claiming to be married to his lord father when in truth they have pulled the wool over the late king's eyes.
Love had blinded king Henry into believing his marriage to Katherine of Aragon – Mary's mother – to have been true. And he had wasted twenty-four years on her.

His second wife had been no better, alluring him with the promise of a son. But God had known her to be a deceitful whore, which was why He never did grant her that son she had fervently promised.

It was because of this – their stripped rank of princesses – that his sisters were not to sit with their brother, the king, at the top table under the gold cloth of state.

They were not legitimate royals. And therefore, protocol dictated that they were not to be perceived as such when visiting the royal court.

But Edward loved his sisters. It was the one thing he believed would never change, despite their extreme differences.

For though they weren't as noble, pure, or exceptional as he, Edward believed them to be loyal sisters and subjects.

He would have to marry them off to nobles soon, however. For no matter how much Edward loved them, he could not allow them to remain unwed and uncontrolled as his father had done. God only knows what his late father had been thinking when he had readmitted them to his line of succession.

But of course, it did not matter. For when Edward was eventually to wed, he would produce his own *legitimate* heirs to succeed him.

His sisters would never sit upon his rightful throne, no matter what his father had planned before his death and written in his will.

They may continue to act as princesses in the hope of one day taking his place, but the whole country – and the whole world – knew them for what they truly are.

But their illegitimacy aside, they were also – quite simply – weak women. They wouldn't have the strength that it takes to run an entire realm.

After all, it was called a *king*dom for a reason.

May 1548

"Catherine Parr is with child," Edward Seymour Lord Protector told the king as he sat upon his recently modified new throne.

King Edward had ordered for a copy of his father's great golden throne to be reproduced, the size of the throne being the only alteration to its design. With this new, leaner throne, King Edward no longer sat upon it swamped in the seat's width, but snug and assertive, knowing that he no longer looked too small for his position.

"Your sister, the Lady Elizabeth," Seymour continued, "as well as the Lady Jane Grey, continue to reside with the lady Catherine, though there are reports of a disruption."

Following the death of Henry VIII, Edward's sister Elizabeth had been taken in by their stepmother, to reside with her and Edward's uncle, Thomas. This had quickly led to the Lady Jane Grey to be taken in by them as their ward as well, so that she and Elizabeth may continue their education together.

King Edward frowned, "A disruption?"

Seymour swallowed and shifted from one foot to the other uncomfortably, "It is said that the Lady Catherine is not taking well to pregnancy. And that she has decided to send the lady Elizabeth away, to lessen her stressors."

"She sends my sister away," young Edward summarised, "But Jane Grey continues among her household?"

Seymour nodded, averting his brown eyes from the king, hoping to move on without further question.

But the king continued, "Why is my sister sent away, and not the Lady Grey?"

The Lord Protector inhaled deeply, "It is said that," he paused briefly, trying to think of how best to word his reply to deflect his brother's connection from himself, "...Catherine Parr's lord husband has taken an inappropriate interest in the Lady Elizabeth."

The young king's eyebrows shot up, "I know who her lord husband is, uncle," Edward said, "You need not mask his relation to you."

Seymour bowed in apology and the boy king sighed.

"What inappropriate behaviour has occurred?" Edward asked.

"Nothing specific has been reported," Seymour lied, choosing not to mention his brother's early morning antics in the young Elizabeth's bedroom.

August 1548

In the months that followed, Edward saw little of anyone he cared about.

His sister Mary had decided to return to her house in the country, her Catholic beliefs continuing strong despite her knowledge of Edward's distaste of it.

His former stepmother, Catherine, had not been enjoying her pregnancy, reports of her ill health being heard throughout all of London despite having sent one of her wards away to, supposedly, alleviate her stress.

Archbishop Cranmer was holed up in his study with a committee of six bishops and six other humanists for days on end. With Cranmer's leadership, they would continue busy for the following months with what would be the country's next step towards eradicating Catholicism.

And though the king and his uncle Edward Seymour had spent nearly every day together since his coronation, the young boy had not bonded with his maternal uncle on any other level than that of king and advisor.

It left Edward with little company besides that of his pet Spaniel, and his friend Barnaby, whom – though he enjoyed his company greatly – he realised had become less focused on his education and more interested in pursuing ladies.

"I urge you to remember your studies, Barnaby," the king told his friend.

At the age of thirteen, over two years older than his king, Barnaby had recently discovered the joys of the opposite gender, writing romantic poems to several ladies of the court he had taken a fancy to, whether they be older than he or not.

"It's when they avert their gaze shyly, Your Grace," Barnaby explained, "That's when you know you're in with a chance."

"You speak so boldly," Edward protested, "Many of the ladies you trifle with are already promised to others."

Barnaby shrugged, "Promised is not wed."

Edward shook his head, his chest growing heavy with the continued topic of women and Barnaby's pursuit of them.

"The lady Richards was so good as to let me caress the tops of her bosom yesterday," Barnaby confessed then, his lopsided grin pulled brazenly across his face.

Edward cringed, "She is but eleven years old!"

Barnaby raised his eyebrows, "You wouldn't know it from where I was standing," he said mischievously, but noticing his friend's unimpressed expression, Barnaby laughed.

"Come now, Edward," he said as he squeezed his friend's shoulder, "There is no harm in this kind of talk. You're a man! And a king! We have needs."

Edward raised one blond eyebrow, "It is not something I have time to consider," he said.

But it was a lie.

Edward had considered it.

He had been considering it for what felt like a very long time. And yet, when he did find himself thinking of kissing, touching, and laying with someone – though he had *tried* again and again to think of it – he could never envision a lady with firm breasts and smooth skin.

In fact, the very idea of it turned his stomach.

He looked at his friend then as two young girls walked past them, giggling inanely from behind their hands.

Barnaby followed them with his seafoam-green gaze, and when he noticed Edward staring at him, he raised his eyebrows, "Those two seemed keen."

Edward narrowed his eyes at him. And Barnaby's impish smile disappeared.

"What is it, Edward?" he asked, noticing his friend's irked mood for the first time.

Edward shook his head, "Nothing."

"It seems like more than nothing," Barnaby replied, placing a hand on Edward's shoulder, which caused a tingling to coarse through Edward's entire body.

He shoved Barnaby's hand off his shoulder like he'd been burned, "Don't!" he ordered.

Barnaby frowned, "Edward, I don't understand. What's the matter?"

Edward was seeing red, his inability to easily conjure up a woman's naked body without feeling revolted disturbed him beyond understanding, and he suddenly wanted nothing more than to be able to talk about girls as easily as Barnaby did.

"Nothing is the matter!" he insisted.

"Edward –"

"NO!" the king replied angrily then, surprising even himself, "It's 'Your Majesty' to you! It's 'Your Majesty' to everyone! Know your place, goddammit!"

September 1548

"Catherine Parr has died of childbed fever, Your Majesty," Lord Protector Edward Seymour informed his nephew just days after news had been delivered of the birth of a healthy baby girl. King Edward looked up from his journal, his eyes wide with shock at the tragic news. He sat back in his seat and lay his quill down gently, careful not to blot ink onto the page.

"Died," he repeated, but it wasn't a question.

Edward Seymour nodded.

"The same way my mother died."

Again, Seymour nodded.

King Edward shook his head slowly, as if he were struggling to believe it.

Then he picked up his quill once again and sat forward, readying himself to continue writing.

Seymour's eyebrows knitted together briefly, his nephew's lack of reaction to his former stepmother's death confusing the older man.

He was about to turn on his heel and exit the room when the king suddenly spoke.

"What is it with all these useless women?" he said, unapologetically, his eyes showing no emotion as he looked up at his uncle.

"None," the king continued, "Not one, seems to be able to fulfil their duty to their husbands without one failure or more."

"Your Majesty?" Seymour said, making his inability to comprehend quite clear.

"Parr," the king replied as though in explanation, "She was a brilliant, educated woman. Intelligent. Perhaps the most educated of all my father's wives. And yet, even she was unable to – not only birth a worthy child, a son – but she was also unable to simply *survive* the delivery."

Edward Seymour only blinked, so stunned was he by the boy's words.

"Childbirth," the king continued, "It is a woman's *one function*. And though she was brilliant, it seems in the end, she was just as useless as any other one of my father's former wives."

Chapter 10

5th January 1549

"The Edwardian Injunctions were not enough," archbishop Cranmer explained to the Lord Protector.
It was the eve before Parliament's announcement of their decision whether or not to pass the king's newest Act.
But of course they would pass it. Cranmer and Edward Seymour had made sure of it…
"The king's Act of Uniformity," Cranmer continued, "is the next logical step towards the official introduction of Protestant doctrine and practice into England and Wales."
Seymour nodded, "You don't have to convince me, archbishop," he said, "With this we will be able to establish our Book of Common Prayer and replace the Roman Rite. Latin will no longer be the sole language of God."

The Act of Uniformity was passed, and with it, the Book of Common Prayer was introduced as the new official book of prayer, replacing the various Latin rites with this one book in the English vernacular. To be used by everyone.
This Act mandated that the entire realm follow the religious practices outlined in the new Book of Common Prayer, and Parliament ordered the clergy to comply with the changes within one year.
Failure to do so would lead to punishment, ranging from life imprisonment to death.
The original committee had been divided in the Book's support, the bishops in the House of Lords only barely voting for its adoption.

But nonetheless, with its passing the English liturgical tradition of nearly a thousand years had been altogether overturned as though it had never been, leading the people of England towards a religious unrest of such scale they had never before experienced.

There was too much going on behind closed doors, too many individuals competing for their own slice of power.
Every day, King Edward received letters from one corner of the country or another with never-ending issues.
Some arrived containing threats of an uprising in several counties to the king's new Protestant laws.
Others were from his uncle, Thomas Seymour, attempting to persuade the young king that he did not need a Lord Protector, or that *he* would be better suited for the job than his brother Edward Seymour.
And yet others warning the king of Thomas Seymour's inappropriate relationship with his fourteen-year-old sister Elizabeth.
"He wants to *marry* the lady Elizabeth?" Lord Protector Edward Seymour asked, his brow furrowed in confusion, feigning having no previous knowledge of his brother's disturbed plans for power.
There was silence around the council chamber as all eyes turned to the young king.
King Edward was but eleven-years-old, hardly old enough to marry himself, but his word mattered when it came to his sisters' marriages, for they were still his successors – no matter how he felt about that fact.
The blonde-haired, grey-eyed young king looked from his uncle Edward Seymour to the other bearded men before him, one by one staring at him, awaiting his ruling.

"Well," he said, his voice cracking, and he quietly damned puberty. He cleared his throat and tried again, "He is, of course, *not* to marry my sister."

Edward Seymour banged his hand onto the wooden table, "Precisely. The king has ruled it so."

"What makes him think it would even be considered?" said the Lord Protector's new private secretary, William Cecil.

Edward Seymour raised one dark eyebrow and looked down at the paperwork before him, "He claims the lady is in love with him," and he sat down in his chair, his interest in the conversation about his brother now gone, "Let us discuss other matters, Your Majesty–"

"Does he not wish to marry the king to his ward, the Lady Jane Grey, too?" John Dudley duke of Northumberland said, interrupting the Lord Protector, and he shot Edward Seymour a sly sideways glance.

Edward Seymour narrowed his eyes at him but then turned his attention back to the boy king, "Your Majesty should consider a bride from a foreign land, to strengthen England against invasion."

"Your Majesty should do what is best for Protestant England," Dudley interjected once more, to which another advisor, Henry Grey – Jane Grey's father – nodded, "Jane Grey is a Protestant, and as cousin to the king she is of noble birth."

Henry Grey looked hopefully at the king then, his mind wandering to the arrangement he and Thomas Seymour had come to months ago, that Henry Grey would allow Thomas wardship of his daughter, Jane, if he promised in return that Jane and King Edward would be betrothed.

"A foreign princess would bring with her a substantial dowry as well as an alliance," William Cecil added, to which many nodded.

"The Lady Jane Grey," Henry Grey piped up, his eyes darting to-and-fro self-consciously, "My daughter, Your Majesty...has my Lord Admiral Thomas Seymour broached the topic of her with Your Majesty?"

King Edward blinked at Henry Grey, then at his Lord Protector.

"The Lady Grey," young Edward said, as though he were trying to remember.

His uncle, Edward Seymour, scoffed then, "Is this some promise my brother made you, my lord?" he asked, his lopsided smirk suggesting the idea as ludicrous.

The members of the Privy Council began their usual bickering, and the little king sighed, resting his hairless chin onto his closed fist, and watched through bored eyes as the grown men before him argued like little children.

"Gentlemen," he said, but no one paid any attention.

"Gentlemen!" a voice called from across the table, and all the men turned to look at the Lord Protector, "the king wishes to speak."

King Edward stood from his throne, "The matter of my bride may wait! I wish to discuss the country's reception of the Book of Common Prayer."

And with that the councilmen settled into their seats once again, eager to tell their king that England's path to a fully reformed country was well and truly underway.

While, in reality, those who continued to practice Catholicism persisted in their distaste for the king's new changes. And as some planned their Prayer Book Rebellion – as threatened in several letters – others awaited the rise of their Catholic princess, the king's eldest sister, Mary Tudor.

10th January 1549

Much like the bishops in the Houses of Lords, the people of largely Catholic religious loyalty had not been pleased with the replacement of their Latin Bibles for the English Book of Common Prayer.
And as the king had been warned, many of his people had rallied against its publication, thousands of Catholics rising in uproar against their young king, in the hope of presenting their discontent to their sovereign.

"The number of rebels joining the Prayer Book Rebellion in Cornwall and Devon is growing at an alarming rate," the king's advisor John Dudley informed the eleven-year-old king, "the emissary Your Majesty sent to quell the disturbance is finding it impossible to raise local support, and they send pleas of aid from their king."

"Do we have the men?" the young king asked, his grey eyes wide with trepidation.
Dudley raised his chin, "Our military force is weak. But we have had word that they have also beseeched mercenary aid from Italy and Burgundy."

"Will Europe send aid?" the king asked as he fought hard to sound brave, while inside he was shaking.

"We have had no reports yet," Dudley replied, "But hope to get fresh news soon."

"If Europe does not send aid," Edward said quietly, "Will these rebels storm London?"
Dudley licked his lips, "They are Catholics, Your Majesty."
Edward nodded; he had his answer.
The rebels were out for his blood.

*

By the grace of God, Italy and Burgundy did send reinforcements for England's defence against their own rebels, and the king emerged victorious.

Due to the threat to Edward's reign, the order was given to slaughter the protesters, which led to a day-long battle in the name of the king. And the five-thousand common folk armed with pitchforks and knives were no match for the eight-thousand European mercenaries.

Several local priests who had incited this uprising were hung in chains outside their own church tower, while any captured rebels were swiftly executed for treason.

And so, the Prayer Book Rebellion had been squashed. And it would be remembered as the most traumatic event in that region's history since the Black Death that had affected it in 1340, over two-hundred years prior.

"They were blinded by Rome's darkness," the young king said some days later, as though he had done them a favour by ordering their deaths, "And in any case, they were peasants, claiming to know more about God than I, their anointed king!"

"It is not only peasants, Your Majesty," John Dudley replied, "Many Catholic nobles continue ruffled by the new changes."

"I have removed their superstitious images of Saints," the king said in his own defence, "I have disallowed the use of rosary beads. If these small trinkets are what Catholics deem necessary to speak to God, then they truly are blinded. The removal of these heretical items will *ease* their path to God. They were mere obstacles. Without these obstacles, my people will hear God more clearly."

John Dudley and Henry Grey bowed their heads in agreement when Edward Seymour rose from his seat at the council table, suggesting another matter in need of addressing.

He cleared his throat, visibly disturbed by what he was about to say, and King Edward felt the beginnings of a headache taking form behind his eyes.

"We have received a letter from your sister, the Lady Mary," he said as he unfolded the paper, "In it she claims that Your Majesty is 'too young to have an opinion on religious doctrine', and that the Book of Common Prayer is heretical and ungodly." The king's cheeks burned red as his uncle continued to read.

"The lady warns that she has written to her cousin, the Holy Roman Emperor, to send military aid to her should she be disallowed from attending Mass."

The young boy was up in a flash before the Lord Protector had even finished his sentence.

"TRAITOR!" the king screeched, his eyebrows glowing red as his anger spread all over his face, "She has threatened her king and country with this letter, and directly discredited my authority by continuing to attend Mass! I should have her arrested! More noble lords and ladies than she have been punished for much less!"

It was true. Since the Act of Uniformity had been passed by Parliament, many people – whether highborn or low – had been imprisoned or executed for their disagreement with the king's new laws, the Prayer Book Rebellions being but one of many disturbing developments of the king's Protestant introductions.

"This could amount to a war," the Lord Protector said, addressing the council as he placed a hand on the king's slender shoulder and gently pushed him back down onto his throne.

The king did not protest, yet many members of the council looked at one another, uncomfortable with Edward Seymour's blatant snub of their young king.

"If we do not appease the Lady Mary in this," he went on, "England could be faced with a war with Spain, and we are not strong enough to fight back," his piercing eyes searched the faces of the king's advisors.

"Over this matter of religion there really cannot be any exception," John Dudley replied calmly, "The Lady Mary has always been stubborn," to which he looked around the table and observed as some of the older members of the Privy Council nodded in agreement, "She and her mother enjoyed holding an axe over our heads of the power of Spain during Henry VIII's reign. And yet they never came to Katherine of Aragon's rescue, so why should we fear Spain now, over this?"

"Because," Edward Seymour replied as he pressed his thumb and forefinger into the corners of his eyes in frustration, "The king is but eleven years old. He has no betrothed and certainly no heir to follow him soon. The Tudor line is weak!"

At that, King Edward dropped his gaze in embarrassment, his young age and apathy towards marriage causing a knot of guilt to form in his stomach.

"We must contain our people and avoid an invasion at all costs," Seymour continued, "Even if the chance of it going forward is slim, the repercussions of a war with Spain now would be too vast."

The room fell silent for a moment as they awaited their Lord Protector's decision.

"I cannot risk it," he finally said as he shook his head in defeat, "I shall write to the Lady Mary and to King Charles V with my decision. For now, we must allow the Lady Mary to pray as she wishes. And when our king has created a powerful alliance through his marriage with a foreign princess, then we will be strong enough to hold off a Spanish army if the Holy Roman Emperor does indeed wish to fight for his cousin's right to pray as a Catholic."

John Dudley nodded slowly in agreement but watched through narrowed eyes as the Lord Protector quivered visibly at the slightest threat of invasion. And as he leaned back slowly in his seat, he began to see Edward Seymour in a new light, one he had not noticed when he had voted for him as Lord Protector two years prior.

Now, he saw him as nothing more than a coward.

"My sister has me perturbed," the king said to archbishop Cranmer some days later as they sat opposite one another playing chess.

"Her letter?" Cranmer asked casually.

Edward nodded, "And her open disrespect of me, her king."

Cranmer nodded slowly before making his move on the chessboard, opening up the possibility of victory for Edward.

Edward fell for it and made his move, "Checkmate," he said with a grin, to which Cranmer slumped in his seat in feigned defeat.

As they rearranged the board for another game, Edward continued, "I hold my sister in high regard," he admitted, "She has always shown me love and kindness, and despite our differences, I do love her the most."

Cranmer stared at his king, allowing his silence to encourage more admittances from the young boy.

Edward looked up into Cranmer's face, who quickly altered his expression to one of sympathy.

"Is it possible to love someone who so openly disrespects their king?" Edward asked his mentor quietly after making his first move on the chessboard.

Cranmer inhaled deeply as he thought of his reply, for this very answer could mark a pivotal turning point in the boy's life in relation to the future of the country.

The Lady Mary was the young king's heir, in accordance with the laws of Henry VIII's will – though it was of course highly improbable that she would ever inherit the throne. The king being young and healthy, with the prospect of a marriage and heirs in the near future, meaning that the Catholic daughter of Katherine of Aragon would likely never sit upon the throne of England.

However, the young king's love for her was dangerous. And in that slim possibility that Edward VI would – like his father before him – struggle to conceive a male heir, it would be imperative to make sure Edward's newfound discontent with his Catholic sister to be allowed to continue.

And perhaps, even, to thrive…

Cranmer made his move on the board.

"My king," Cranmer said slowly as he sat forward, his eyes shining with exaggerated pity for Edward, which he knew would only aggravate the hot-headed boy on the topic of his sister's disrespect, "I believe it is noble indeed to hold onto the love you feel for your Catholic sister. It shows that you are a great and forgiving king – a true and virtuous young man!" he cleared his throat then, as though pondering whether or not to speak further. But then he did.

"However," he continued as he watched Edward move his pawn, "I believe it is *imperative* that you clamp down on her insolence if you wish to quash the growing religious unrest in your country."

Edward frowned, unsure how one lady's continued devotion to her religion could impact the entire realm.

"She may be a bastard," Cranmer went on as he moved his own black pawn, "But she is the daughter of the much-loved Katherine of Aragon. The Lady Mary is, simply by *existing*, setting an example for all other Catholics. And if she is allowed to stand up to her king in this matter of religion…well, so will the entire Catholic people believe they can."

Edward blinked and then nodded slowly, taking his turn, moving his bishop, "So, you believe Mary is a threat to my country, and my reign?"

Cranmer sighed with exaggerated shame, "I believe," he said tactfully, as he took his turn on the chessboard, "That the Lady Mary knows of your love for her. And she is using it to her advantage to control you."

Edward frowned midway through making his move, his cheeks pinkening with humiliation.

Cranmer picked up his rook then, placing it in blatant harm's way and pretending not to notice. Edward moved his queen and victoriously knocked over Cranmer's king, to which Cranmer *tsked* at himself for his sham defeat, before sitting forward and looKing Edward in the eyes.

"Do not allow others to control you, Your Majesty," he said.

16th January 1549

Edward was exhausted.

The occurrences over the last two weeks had been nothing short of disaster upon disaster and he felt as though he were being pulled by so many people in countless different directions.

He was young, but he had been prepared for push backs from the Catholic people, his advisors had warned him of as much. However, he had not been prepared for actual rebellions to ensue, or for his beloved sister Mary to go against him so disturbingly.

But he had been even less prepared for the scandal regarding his sister Elizabeth and his uncle, Thomas Seymour.

It was all too much, and Edward was beginning to understand why his father never had had time to see him throughout his childhood. If this was what being a king was like, Edward wouldn't be surprised if the stress of it all would one day lead him to an early grave.

"I shall retire to my chambers," the king announced as he sat slumped against the back of his throne, "You may continue your merriment," he added, glad to allow the court to continue enjoying the banquet and dancing in the great hall.

"Shall I accompany you, Your Grace?" the Lord Protector asked, to which the king couldn't help but roll his eyes.

"No, uncle," he said, "Barnaby will come with me."

"Boy!" the Lord Protector called to the table adjacent to the king's top table. He snapped his fingers at Barnaby, "Go with the king."

Edward shook his head at his uncle's rashness, his action and tone having been entirely unnecessary.

But Barnaby was not troubled by it. He looked up from his plate of food and stood, still chewing the last spoonful he had managed to squeeze into his mouth.

The two young men – followed by one guard and the king's pet Spaniel – left the great hall together, the sound of music and laughter growing fainter the further they walked.

Once they had reached the king's chambers, the guard opened the door for the king and his companion. Then he closed it behind them and took his place guarding the chamber from the outside, the king's pooch having taken himself into the corner of the foyer and curled up on his feather cushion for a nap.

"A game of cards, Barnaby?" Edward asked as he sauntered over to the corner of the chambers, where a falcon remained perched lazily in a cage. Edward peered at the falcon for a moment, then walked toward the table by the dimly lit fireplace. The room was warm, the fire in the hearth remaining lit in the king's chambers throughout the day.

Edward removed his furs from his slender shoulders as he took his seat, the warmth from the fireplace proving enough to feel comfortable.

Barnaby kept on watching Edward from a few steps away as his friend folded his furs over the back of his chair before sitting down in it elegantly. He observed as Edward picked up the pack of cards on the table and began to shuffle the deck carefully, then dealt out two hands with a graceful flick of his wrist.

Barnaby approached then, to which Edward glanced up, smiling at him briefly. The falcon squawked idly from behind them, breaking the silence, and a flicker of a thought swiftly crossed Edward's face like a shadow, as if the falcon had reminded him of something. He forced his smile to fade, applying instead a look of casual nonchalance.

Barnaby narrowed his eyes briefly, wondering – as he had done for some months now – what continued to trouble Edward so…

The older boy fanned out the cards in his hands, noting Edward followed suit, but not before stealing another glance at Barnaby yet again.

He had noticed his friend stealing glances at him throughout the years. But lately and more often, Barnaby had felt eyes on him on more than one occasion, only to turn and find Edward quickly looking away or pretending to be looking past him.

Barnaby had thought it odd, to say the least. And in recent months he had come to realise that perhaps there was more to the king's persistent disinterest in girls than mere lack of 'time for such things', as the king had claimed.

Barnaby had tried to show Edward what he was missing. He had often spoken of the soft, doughy feel of a girl's breast, of the warmth between their thighs.

But Edward had shaken his head and cringed each time.

Barnaby had believed, for a time, that perhaps the king was yet too young to enjoy the female form. After all, Barnaby knew that even he himself was a little more eager than many of his peers – and he was a whole two years older than the king to boot.

However, Barnaby was not naïve. He had seen enough girls pining over him to know a longing look when he saw one.

But to receive such looks from a boy – and the *king* – was an entirely unique situation.

And with each lingering look of late, Barnaby was becoming more and more convinced that…despite King Henry VIII's efforts to produce a male heir to further his line, it seemed he had unknowingly produced a son who had no interest in laying with females.

The falcon shrilled lazily in his cage behind him.

"Another hand?" Edward asked upon having won the game, pulling his friend out of his own thoughts.

Barnaby only nodded in response and handed over his losing cards.

Their fingers brushed then as Edward's slender fingers took the cards from Barnaby's outstretched hand. And though they had barely touched, a sudden jolt ran up both of their hands, and they pulled away from one another self-consciously.

Edward dropped the deck of cards he had been holding, the pack making a low thump as they fell face down onto the wooden table. And yet it might as well have been as loud as a clap of thunder, for the two boys jumped up from their seats as though they'd been burned.

"What are you doing?" Barnaby asked, his voice rising an octave.

"What?" Edward asked, unable to meet his friend's eyes, "We are playing cards."

Barnaby didn't reply right away, his heart was beating too wildly, and his words formed a lump in his throat.

"I like girls," Barnaby croaked out after a moment, his green eyes blazing with fear that he had misspoken.
Edward met his friend's agitated gaze then as all the blood from his body rushed down to his feet, and he felt as though the ground was about to collapse from underneath him.
"What?" the king muttered, "Why do you say that?"
"Because you – Your Grace…I see the looks you give me," Barnaby replied in a stuttering gush of words, "Y—you do not like discussing girls with me, you haven't so much as kissed one…"
Edward swallowed hard as his vision blurred, "There is nothing wrong with me – " he whispered.
Suddenly, there was a loud bark from outside the king's chambers, followed quickly by a deafening *bang* and a yelp.
Edward's falcon shrieked then, flapping its wings wildly in fright, feathers flying as it knocked against the metal cage.
The two boys straightened up and turned to stare at the door, frozen in shock, their conversation adjourned.
"Wh –" Edward began, but before he could even form his question the door swung open, bashing against the stone wall, and causing the two young men to flinch.
The king's own uncle, Thomas Seymour, staggered in then as a commotion in the distance grew louder.
"Uncle…" the boy king started to say, before Thomas began waving the gun in his hand around the room.
"Nice," Thomas Seymour mumbled approvingly as he looked up at the beautifully carved ceiling featuring the Tudor rose.
Then he locked eyes with his nephew, "Come with me, boy," he said, waving his gun as though Edward ought to follow him.
Barnaby grabbed the king by the wrist then and pulled him behind him protectively, puffing his chest out assertively towards the older and taller man.

Just then, the metal clanging and shouting of the guards' quick approach engulfed them.

"Help!" they heard one call from the foyer, "Murder!"

Edward frowned briefly, *Murder?*

Thomas lunged forward suddenly and shoved Barnaby to the floor with just the push of one hand, then he reached to grab the king by the arm.

Edward evaded him just as dozens of guards burst through the open doors of the king's chambers and his falcon continued shrieking and bashing nervously around in its too-small cage.

The guards had all drawn their swords and were edging carefully towards Seymour as he turned and held up his hands. He knew that, even with a gun, he did not have a chance to shoot his way out of this.

Barnaby scrambled up from the floor and, with Edward, hurried towards the guards, squeezed past them, and fled out the door.

"Your Majesty!" they heard Thomas Seymour call from behind them just as Edward Seymour, archbishop Cranmer and John Dudley came running around the corner.

"Your Majesty!" they all called as they raced towards Edward and Barnaby.

"Don't look," Barnaby whispered beside Edward then as he stared wide-eyed towards the far corner of the foyer.

Edward, despite having been told not to, followed his friend's gaze, and gasped.

His beloved Spaniel – a gift from his uncle Thomas himself – lay on its side, its tongue lolling out of its open mouth and its body half hanging off the side of its feathered cushion, in a puddle of its own blood.

Murder!

The shrill noise of his frightened falcon's screeches continued in the background above all the other raucous.

"Your Majesty!" Thomas Seymour called from behind them again, this time in unison with the calls from the men running towards them.

And before Edward knew it, his head was tolling with the buzz of many different shouts, screeches and heavy footsteps, all calling and pulling him in different directions yet again, as though he were a prized stag hung from the rafters, to be torn from limb by limb for their sustenance.

Chapter 11

"Ought we not await the king himself before you begin the meeting?" John Dudley asked rhetorically, nodding his head at the empty throne at the head of the council table.

The Lord Protector sighed heavily, "He is not attending," he said.

The men looked at one another in silence, many of them watching Seymour through narrowed eyes.

The Lord Protector and self-appointed Duke of Somerset Edward Seymour, had begun to irk many within the king's council, his spinelessness in relation to the Lady Mary's threat having stood out as the wrong course of action. But above even that, many had begun to dislike the way in which he would openly disregard the young king's ruling for his own.

And that was not what his position was in aid of.

As Lord Protector, they had voted Seymour in to be the young king's guide, to show him the path he ought to take but not to force his decision for him. Since, ultimately, the *king* was the king – not Edward Seymour.

"The Lord Admiral's plan had been to kidnap the king," Lord Protector Edward Seymour explained then, breaking the silence, in a futile attempt to defend his foolish younger brother, "He sent the guard on a wayward errand to gain privacy with the king, but then the king's Spaniel must have spooked him by barking and Thomas shot it to quieten it. But he did not mean *the king* any harm!"

"Kidnap?" John Dudley asked, playing dumb, as though he were unaware of the glaringly obvious dispute for power between the Seymour brothers, which had been a rather entertaining topic of gossip throughout the years.

But no one was laughing now, for Thomas Seymour's pathetic attempts at attaining power had finally gone too far.

Edward Seymour sighed, "There is nothing I can say in my brother's defence that will appease any of us, or the king," he said, "We all now know the lengths he would seek to go to obtain power over this council and the king."

"But, he is the king's uncle!" Henry Grey added in a last-ditch effort for leniency since his daughter, Jane Grey, continued to be Thomas' ward; and Grey still hoped Thomas would somehow manage to arrange a union between his daughter and the king, "Surely the king ought to have a say on the matter?"

John Dudley snorted a laugh, aware of Grey's personal plotting but frankly indifferent to him entirely, "I'm sure if the king were recovered enough from the ordeal to attend this meeting, his uncle would be walking the scaffold already."

And though he had been addressing Grey's remark, Dudley made a point of looking directly into Edward Seymour's eyes when he spoke.

February 1549

King Edward was of course shaken by the reckless kidnapping attempt by his uncle. But it was the topic Barnaby had broached before the chaos had ensued that persisted in the boy's mind.

I like girls.

You haven't so much as kissed one.

His friend's words echoed in his mind on a loop.

His friend.

Would he even want to keep being his friend?

"What if my uncle heard us?" Edward asked frantically.

Barnaby frowned and shook his head, "He didn't," he reassured.

"What if he *did!?*"

Barnaby looked down at the ground, searching his mind, then he took a step towards his friend and took Edward's hands in his.

They were clammy with sweat and worry.

"Edward," he said quietly as he forced his king to make eye contact with him, "I shall never tell a soul."

Edward looked up and met his friend's steady gaze. He swallowed his words of protest and nodded, "I know."

And he did. He had always known where his friend's loyalties lay.

"But," Barnaby continued then, to which Edward couldn't help but flinch, "If your uncle did hear…do you trust *him* to keep your secret?"

I see the looks you give me.
There's nothing wrong with me…

Edward suddenly turned from his friend, tearing his hands free of his and pressed his fingers hard against his forehead.

He groaned in anger, fear and frustration, aggravated by the weight of his secret.

"Leave me," he ordered from over his shoulder, embarrassed still to have Barnaby know of his feelings for him.

He balled his hands into fists as soon as the door closed behind him, then thumped himself repeatedly on his forehead, hoping to banish all thoughts of Barnaby and his accursed ability to have such a hold over the King of England's thoughts and feelings.

If only Edward knew, that of all the people at court, Barnaby was the only one who had never even aspired to such an influence over him.

March 1549

Thomas Seymour was imprisoned, having been accused of not only attempting to kidnap and potentially harm the King of England, but also of thirty-two other treasonous crimes – one of which included planning to marry the king's sister in secret in an attempt to place himself on the throne in the king's stead.

"Your sister Elizabeth has been questioned, Your Grace," the Lord Protector informed the young king, "She denies any involvement and so does her governess, the Lady Katherine Ashley."

Edward nodded slowly, only half listening. His beloved sister Mary was already betraying him in matters of religion. Surely his other sister would not also attempt to deceive him.

"What evidence is there of their relationship?" the king asked half-heartedly.

"None, Your Majesty," Edward Seymour replied, to which John Dudley scoffed, now openly affronting Seymour's authority.

"See to it that she is questioned again," the king said, "If she is made to repeat her story she is bound to slip up if there is any truth to my uncle's plans of marriage."

Seymour bowed his head and quit the council chamber to convey the message to the king's councilmember, Tyrwhit, who was questioning the Lady Elizabeth at her residence in Cheshunt.

John Dudley took a seat closer to the king upon the Lord Protector's exit, licking his lips beneath his dark beard.

"It has been quite the tumultuous start to your reign, Your Majesty," he remarked casually, though the statement was of course extremely loaded.

Edward looked up, his grey eyes lacking lustre for more than the reasons known to his council.

When the king did not reply, John Dudley continued, "This year alone has been marked by economic and social unrest. And we mustn't forget the expensive war in Scotland which led to naught."

"What is your point, Dudley," the king asked, exhaling heavily through his nose, unable to muster enough strength to even attempt to decipher the hidden meaning behind his advisor's words. For a hidden meaning, Edward knew, there was.

"My point, my king," Dudley said quietly as the other advisors pretended not to hear, though they had all agreed with Dudley's plan to remove Seymour from power, "Is that it seems your Lord Protector is failing miserably in his position."

Edward met the older man's sharp gaze, unsure on how to respond.

Dudley was not wrong. His uncles had both been reaching high since his ascension to the throne.

Edward had always taken his Lord Protector's guidance at face value, since he had told him it was what his late father had wanted.

Had he been played for an immature fool?

"My father appointed the Duke of Somerset as my Lord Protector," the young king said with a hint of self-doubt.

John Dudley breathed a laugh through his nose then, "Oh my most gracious king…is that what he told you?"

May 1549

They had not needed evidence or a confession from the Lady Elizabeth to convict Thomas Seymour, for his thirty-three counts of treason against the king were cause enough to have him executed.

He was beheaded, his head being cropped from his body with not one but two blows of the axe.

The king's sister, Elizabeth, was allowed to resume her mundane life at her home in Hertfordshire, cleared of any suspicion of betrayal to her king.

But the king's other sister's betrayal in the matter or religion continued as a headache to Edward and his council.

"Send this letter to the Lady Mary," the Lord Protector told his messenger before turning back to address the members of the Privy Council, "In it I have written with absolute clarity that neither the Lady Mary, nor anyone, ought to be excused from the king's new laws."

The councilmen nodded their heads, "You saw reason then, my lord," they mumbled, remembering Seymour's past decision to allow the Lady Mary to pray as she saw fit until England was strengthened enough to withhold an attack from Spain.

But John Dudley was not convinced. He saw right through Seymour's stiff posture and the way he shuffled the documents before him awkwardly.

There would be more to that letter, Dudley was sure of it.

He just wasn't sure of what.

As it turned out, the Lord Protector's letter had stated that the Lady Mary would not be exempt or allowed to attend Mass as she had always done throughout her life. The new laws of the land were to be obeyed. By everyone.

What it had *also* said, however, was that while she must follow the king's new laws, there would not be any investigation made to what may or may not be occurring within her household at Hunsdon House.

Edward Seymour saw this as the only way to appease both sides and to avoid the possibility of war with Spain.

He knew that it was an unlikely probability that the Lady Mary's cousin, King Charles V of Spain, were to send military aid to her on this – or any – matter. John Dudley had been right in the fact that Spain had not even aided Katherine of Aragon all those years ago when Henry VIII had been dragging her reputation through the mud.

And yet, Edward Seymour also knew that something had needed to be done, for even the slimmest chance of threat to the country while the king was but twelve years old, would have been the end of his Protestant rule.

Henry VIII had left the country in a military and economic crisis, one that England had not yet been able to claw its way out of.

John Dudley, as a mere member of the Privy Council, would not be fully aware of the extent of this. And he would never understand the difficult position Seymour was in, trying to juggle the matter of religion, as well as trying to rule a financially broken country alongside a boy who had not yet grown a single chin hair.

John Dudley would never understand the pressures of this role. Edward Seymour only hoped that one day soon, his efforts to maintain peace would be recognised, and that he would be hailed for his abilities as Lord Protector.

Little did he know, that while he was patting himself on the back for his apparent successes, the members of his council had turned against him and looked to another to take his position as the young king's chief advisor.

December 1549

Edward Seymour had governed as king in all but name for three years, but his increasingly stubborn and over-bearing

attitude had begun to alienate the very men whose backing he had initially needed to attain the title of Lord Protector.
And the rest of the council had now had enough.

"We are in agreement then?" Dudley asked the men before him, "Seymour has proven himself incompetent following the many failures and uprisings towards the king's new laws."
They all nodded their heads, including even William Cecil, who had only achieved status as member of the Privy Council through employment by Edward Seymour.

"He and his brother have tried to reach too high," Dudley concluded, "And despite his brother's ending, Edward Seymour continues to want to reach higher still."
Dudley sighed and shook his head, "We must collectively force him out and present to the young king all his downfalls."

"Will the king listen to reason?" Henry Grey asked, his moustache quivering with each word.
John Dudley turned to fix his gaze on Grey, and though he had always believed him to be a spineless and weak-minded man, Dudley was glad for him to have asked that question.

"I have the king's ear," Dudley admitted, "And he has given me enough reason to believe that he, too, has had enough of Seymour's overstepping."

King Edward had not needed much persuasion, for he had had his eyes opened to the error in his uncle's ways. And shortly after Edward Seymour's forceful removal from the king's Privy Council, John Dudley was assigned to take his place.
The former Lord Protector was sent to the Tower, imprisoned for his crimes of ambition, vainglory, entering into rash wars, enriching himself with the king's treasury, and more, which King Edward read out to him personally.
And the newly established king's council began to attempt to right Edward Seymour's wrongs.

They – with John Dudley as newly appointed President of the Council – began by clamping down on those who they had believed Edward Seymour to be too lax on during his time in power.

The religious conflict with the king's sister, the Lady Mary, being John Dudley's first order of business.

"I propose we send priests to the Lady Mary at Hunsdon House to get her to convert," John Dudley said, wording his ruling in the form of a suggestion, to give the illusion that it would ultimately be the young king's order.

But really, Dudley was just as power hungry as Seymour had been – he would just be more subtle in his ways.

The young king nodded, "Send them," he agreed, but not before adding his own gift of illumination to his beloved sister, "And I shall send her a collection of Protestant books to aid her understanding. She is clever, for a woman, and I am sure with the right guidance, the Lady Mary shall turn to the light of Protestantism in no time."

His sister's conversion to Protestantism was a hope that lived deeply inside Edward's heart. As his heir should he die childless, Mary held an importance no other woman had ever been graced with in England. And with her stubbornness to see sense, she was threatening the only thing Edward held dear – namely, his faith.

Although, if he were truthful with himself, Protestantism was not the *only* thing he held dear.

And the night of his potential kidnapping, Barnaby had made it clear that his secret was beginning to show.

Edward was nearing thirteen-years-old, a young man. And yet he had not felt that magnetic pull towards a woman the way other boys his age had, supposedly, been starting to feel.

But he had had urges. Tingling sensations all over his body whenever he considered the possibility of laying with someone. And he would wake in the middle of the night with an arousal he could not seem to extinguish unless he touched himself and thought of Barnaby.

The aftermath of it all made him feel ashamed beyond belief, and each time he would lay his head back down on his feather pillow and promise himself that next time he would envision a lady.

Any lady. It did not matter.

But he never did. And each occasion his deceitful body tingled with the sinful need, Edward would think of his friend – a young man, with whom he could never truly be with.

As the teenaged king lay on his back that night, spent after another urgent and uncontrollable demand from his body for release, he considered that perhaps Protestantism *wasn't* the only thing he held dear.

After all, he could not fathom or even consider the possibility of a wedded union with a woman – not even for the production of a Protestant heir, as the very idea of the act made him shudder with disgust.

And if he were willing to throw it all away – his father's hard work, his own – then perhaps Protestantism must not be what he loved the most.

Perhaps what he loved more than even his faith…was Barnaby.

Chapter 12

February 1550

King Henry VIII had done an excellent job at recreating a miniature replica of himself when he created Edward VI.
Though he took after his mother in looks with fair hair and freckles on his nose, Edward was his father's son in temper, impatience, and arrogance.
He let his true colours show once his newly modified council had been reshuffled, and his overbearing uncle Edward Seymour had been imprisoned.
Many believed this to be due to the young king's sudden taste of freedom after escaping under the thumb of his Lord Protector. But in truth, Edward was taking the rage and disgust he felt for himself out on his people and all those around him.
"I don't want to settle this with peace and a betrothal!" Edward bellowed, slamming his hands down on the table as he stood, "Send an army!"
"England is weak, Your Majesty," the newly appointed President of the Council, John Dudley, said, "Militarily drained from the war in Scotland. And France has taken advantage of this when they declared war to take back Boulogne."
Despite the initial attack having been successful, Henry VIII's siege of Boulogne several years prior had been rather a pitiful claim of victory.
Edward saw this now. And he cringed at his younger self berating his wiser tutor, John Cheke, all those years ago.
While the late king had left the city in the good hands of men he had trusted with the order to continue to siege more of France for England, they had failed, but had managed to hold onto Boulogne by the skin of their teeth.

And now the French were warring to take their city back while England's newest king was regarded as being practically still in his cradle.

"We cannot fight off their army with the military standing we currently have," Dudley explained, "We *must* negotiate a peace with the French."

William Cecil, who had recently been appointed Secretary of State to the young Protestant king, nodded his head, his brown hair flopping over his eyes.

He pushed his hair aside, "We may gain more from the loss of Boulogne than from keeping it, Your Highness," he said.

King Edward sat back down, nudging his chin in Cecil's direction for him to go on.

"A peace treaty would put an end to England and France's disdain for one another," Cecil went on, "We could offer Boulogne back to the French without a war, and instead offer it up for ransom."

"Ransom?" King Edward asked more calmly now.

His voice had finally settled after over a year of uncontrollable highs and lows, and it had made him feel more sure of himself.

Dudley raised an eyebrow, "Indeed, Your Grace. By offering the city back for a price, England would avoid a war we cannot win, as well as attain a financial triumph to strengthen our country."

The room went silent while the teenaged king considered this.

"And the betrothal?" he asked while ignoring the lump in his throat, knowing he had to feign interest in a wedded union.

Dudley nodded, "We would cement the treaty with a betrothal to the daughter of king Henry II, the French Princess Elisabeth of Valois."

"She is but a child, is she not?" Edward asked, though he already knew.

"Indeed, Your Majesty," Dudley replied, "There would be no arrangements for the marriage until the girl's twelfth birthday at the earliest."

Edward nodded his head. He would have a few years to get out of the arrangement.

"See to it that the French agree to this," he said, "But make it clear that the King of England is no pushover! I will not take this act of war lightly, nor will I simply hand over Boulogne for pittance!"

"Of course not, Your Majesty," Cecil replied, "We believe a ransom of two-hundred-thousand crowns would make a handsome reward for England."

Edward frowned, "I won't give up my God-given right to Boulogne for that, Cecil! Be serious!"

"My lord?"

Edward shook his long, slim finger in the air, "I won't accept anything less than four-hundred-thousand, Cecil. Make sure the French know they cannot simply walk all over me because of my age! I am my father's son. And it's about time Europe hears about it!"

March 1550

The Treaty of Boulogne was signed.

England received four-hundred-thousand crowns, as well as a perpetual defensive alliance with France, in exchange for the city.

War was avoided. Lives were spared.

And yet somehow, many in England believed the treaty to have been a national disgrace.

"The people see this as a humiliating experience against our traditional enemy, France," William Cecil explained to their teenaged king, "They are calling for John Dudley's position as President of the Council to be revoked."

Edward snorted a laugh as he picked up his golden cup of wine, "The people do not have a say in the matter," he replied.

Cecil bowed his head, showing his agreement.

"A war with France would have bankrupted our country," Dudley added in his defence, "This was the lesser of two evils."

"Spare me the details, Dudley," the king said, "I already know of them."

Dudley bowed at the waist, glad to have his king's approval.

"Besides," Edward continued after taking a sip of his wine, "I am content with your work, councillor. The people may shout their distaste for your advice, but they cannot overrule their king. And as long as I appreciate your input, your position within my council is safe."

The men settled down to continue their council meeting, their minds setting aside the English people's discontent as unimportant.

But unbeknownst to them, the former Lord Protector Edward Seymour, was taking the people's discontent as a sure-fire sign that his return would be welcomed. And he began to devise a plan from within his cell which would see to the end of his usurper John Dudley, and Seymour's reinstatement as the most powerful man in England once more.

April 1550

The following month, Edward Seymour had been released from the Tower by none other than his successor, John Dudley believing his position within the Privy Council solidified enough to allow the king's uncle his liberty.

Unbeknownst to him, Edward Seymour – upon tasting freedom – began implementing the plan he had been hatching for several weeks when word had reached his ears that the people were not best pleased with Dudley.

"My beautiful daughters," Edward Seymour said lovingly as he embraced his youngest daughters Mary and Jane Seymour.

"Welcome, father," Jane, the eldest of the two, said.

Edward kissed her on the top of her blond head, "I am glad to be back."

Later that night, as Edward sat by the roaring fire of his chambers, his wife sitting opposite him at the dining table, his daughters busied themselves with the tasks they had previously had servants for, before their father's downfall.

"I wish to share my plans with you," Edward said to his wife, who looked up from her plate of bread and cheese.

"Plans?" she repeated, unsure of what her husband was referring to.

Seymour nodded, then tugged uneasily at his greying beard, "I have had much time to think while in the Tower," he began, "and the people's discontent with Dudley needs to be taken advantage of."

His wife blinked at him, "The people's discontent? My lord, what are you speaking of?"

Edward turned his head towards his daughter Jane then and snapping his fingers, "Jane!" he called, "Come."

The young girl obeyed and approached, looking from her mother to her father.

"Jane is the key," Edward said with a grin.

Jane looked to her mother in confusion, who looked back with the same puzzled expression on her face.

"Jane is not only pretty," Edward explained, "But clever beyond her years."

"What are you talking about, Edward?" his wife asked then, her face twisted with irritation at his nonsensical ramblings.

Edward Seymour took his daughter's hand in his, "Jane is the key!" he repeated, "She will speak to the king for me. She will infiltrate his mind with positive things about her lord father. And with any luck, not only will I be reinstated into my former position, but if Jane catches the king's eye, then she might well become the next Queen of England."

Jane Seymour, named after her late aunt and former Queen Jane of England, was confused to say the least.
Not only was she but twelve years old and hardly physically mature enough to be of any immediate interest to the king, but she had absolutely no idea *how* she was supposed to regain her father's former glory.
Did her father really think the king would fall for the fairly obvious sudden interest she would have to show him, as well as the extremely awkward positive remarks her father wished for her to spout at King Edward out of the blue?
Jane and the king had no previous rapport. She and he were not of the same station or even of the same social circle…
In fact, Jane could count on one hand how many times she had even spoken to the king. Namely – once.
Had her father lost his senses during his stint in the Tower?
Jane certainly hoped not…but was rather certain that it was a possibility.
Nevertheless, Jane would do her duty by her father. After all, as a girl she was bound to obey and serve. And if her attempt were to lead to her family's rise once more then she would of course do all in her power to achieve it.

It was during a joust the following week that Jane Seymour gained the opportunity to catch the king's eye.
Well, not the *king's* eye specifically, but his best friend, Barnaby's.

She had noticed him smiling at her before, some months ago during a banquet when her father had still been Lord Protector. And he was smiling at her again now, no doubt having thought her repeated glances at the king beside him had been directed at him.

Jane, knowing that to become close to the king's best friend was a sure way to becoming close to the king himself, returned his smile before turning shyly back to observe the joust.

After the event, as the lords and ladies made their way back towards the castle, Jane made sure to catch Barnaby's eye once more, hoping he would see it as an invitation to speak to her.

He did. And Jane was, for the first time, able to witness just how easily influenced young men could be.

"Good day, my lady," Barnaby said, his intensely green eyes shining with mischief.

"Good day, sir," she replied with a quick curtsy, averting her eyes.

"What a glorious day for a stroll," Barnaby said, looking up into the clear sky, "Do you wish to accompany me for a moment in the gardens?"

Jane offered him a pretty smile before meeting his gaze purposefully, "I would indeed," she said.

Barnaby turned to stand beside her and offered her his arm.

"Might I be so bold as to suggest we invite the king?" Jane added sweetly then, "It is such a glorious day, as you have mentioned."

Barnaby's smile twitched slightly, irked to be denied her private company, but he nodded nonetheless.

"Your Majesty," Barnaby called over the many heads of the people making their way over the lawn towards the castle.

King Edward turned to the sound of his friend's voice, and Jane thought she noticed a glitter of something in the king's eye at the sound of Barnaby's voice. Something she could not quite place.

But she pushed her thoughts aside. *No doubt he is but joyful of the day's entertainment.*

The king approached them with a smile on his face, which instantly vanished as he spotted Jane and Barnaby's arms interlinked.

"Barnaby," the king said in greeting, his tone much colder than Jane had expected for his best friend.

"Your cousin has suggested we take a walk in the gardens," Barnaby said, to which Jane cocked her head to one side since a walk had been *his* suggestion, "Do you wish to join us?"

The king's grey-eyed gaze fell to her, to which she smiled prettily and curtsied as low as she could, making sure to maintain eye contact with him throughout, as her mother had informed her men liked.

King Edward watched her as she curtsied, seemingly indifferent to her obvious flirtation.

"Certainly," he said as she straightened up, but then stood on Barnaby's other side, so that Jane was furthest away from him. Upon entering the beautiful gardens, Jane leaned slightly forward as they walked to address the king, hoping to make it clear that while she had initially caught Barnaby's attention, it was the king she wished to speak to.

"What a fantastic joust that was, Your Majesty," she said, smiling brightly.

"Indeed," the king agreed before flashing a quick glance at his friend.

"Lord Neville did especially well today," Jane added, hoping to begin a flow to the conversation.

The king nodded, "Mm."

They walked in silence for a while, the air becoming heavier with each moment that passed as the awkwardness of the situation grew. Though Jane Seymour did not know why.

"May I enquire as to Your Majesty's favourite jouster?" Jane asked, trying one more time to make it clear that it was Edward she wished to speak to.

Edward opened his mouth to speak but then closed it again, frowning.

Jane's eyebrows twitched, "Have I offended Your Grace?" she asked, fully aware now that he did not care to speak with her.

"Not at all, my lady," the king replied half-heartedly.

But then he stopped in his tracks and turned to face them, "Actually, I cannot stay," he said, "I have urgent business to attend to."

And with that, Edward left.

Jane and Barnaby watched him leave, Jane's face creased with confusion.

"Have I done something?" Jane asked Barnaby as she continued to watch the king walk away.

Barnaby looked from Jane to Edward in the distance and sighed.

"No," he admitted rashly, now that he knew Jane hadn't cared for alone time with him after all, "But you are wasting your time if you wish for the king's affection."

Jane faced the older boy, "Oh?" she challenged, crossing her arms before her.

Barnaby observed her defiant stance and laughed, hoping to mask the annoyance he felt for having been used to attain a private moment with the king, "You and every lady are wasting your time with our king," he said, a dark shadow flickering over his face as he realised he had said too much.

Jane only frowned.

"Forgive me, my lady," Barnaby mumbled suddenly, before clearing his throat, "As it turns out, I too have matters to attend to."

And with that Barnaby fled after the king, leaving little Jane Seymour feeling more confused than she had ever felt in her entire life.

"You said what?!" Edward hissed bewilderedly at his friend.

"She won't understand my meaning," Barnaby replied, though the tremor in his voice betrayed his belief in his own words.

"You cannot be serious," Edward said as he began to pace the room, his hands on his head, "Because the girl did not show an interest in you, you decide to put my kingdom in jeopardy?!"

By now, Edward had confessed his feelings for his friend, who had sworn to keep his secret.

It had been an uncomfortable confession for the both of them, to say the least, Barnaby never having known anyone to harbour affections towards another of the same sex.

But he had been accepting of his king and friend, and vowed to preserve his secret, as long as Edward maintained his side of the bargain that he would never overstep their friendship to satisfy his own desires. For Barnaby remained steadfast that he was not like Edward, and that he did not wish to explore the male form in any way, and for no amount of riches.

"She will not understand," Barnaby repeated, confident this time.

But Edward was not listening, "No," he said, "I cannot risk it. I shall have to fix this."

"Father!" Jane called as she entered her family's chambers.

She closed the door behind her and removed her shawl, looking around the empty rooms.

Her father entered then, his face beaming with excitement, "I saw you and the king had an audience? A private meeting in the gardens?"

Jane frowned briefly, "We were not in private," she said, "But yes, we had a moment to speak. But father –"

"Was the king in good cheer?" Edward Seymour asked.

"He seemed rather indisposed," Jane admitted, "I must admit I am quite bemused regarding our encounter."

Her father took her by the hand and led her to the table before taking a seat. His daughter followed suit, her eyebrows creased as she replayed the scene in the gardens in her mind.

"The king's friend expressed the most curious of things to me," Jane said slowly, uncertain if she had understood or even heard correctly, "He said that I, as well as any lady, are wasting our time with the king if we wish for his affection."

Edward Seymour visibly flinched in his seat, his eyebrows knitted so tightly together he looked suddenly ten years older than his fifty years.

"He said that?" he asked, though he knew his Jane would not make things up.

Jane nodded, "What does he mean?" she asked innocently.

But Edward knew. He had suspected as much from the young king.

There had been many signs.

His glee over the failed marriage to the Queen of Scots.

His brief expression of repulsion at the mention of Jane Grey.

His uneven breathing over the years at the approach of his best friend.

"Could it be true?" Edward Seymour mumbled under his breath then as he stood from his seat and walked over to the unlit fireplace.

He pulled at his beard as he stared into the hearth, his frown becoming deeper as he thought.

"What is the meaning of this, father?" Jane asked from behind him, her innocence rendering her completely in the dark to this shocking revelation.

Edward Seymour ignored her as he continued to think how he could spin this new information to his advantage.

And all the while he was unaware that his nephew was spinning his own plot. One where the former Lord Protector and his daughter would be arrested on false charges of attempted murder and executed for their fabricated crimes before they could spread the awful truth that the King of England was a homosexual.

Chapter 13

December 1550

Edward Seymour, his wife, and their daughter Jane were all arrested under the allegation of attempted murder of the President of the Council, John Dudley.
This was the story that was swiftly spreading throughout the country, despite there being no evidence of it.
But without evidence, there could be no guilty conviction, Edward knew this.
The king would have to come up with another crime to ensure his uncle would not walk free.

"I do have it under good authority that the Seymours were planning to marry their daughter to the king," Dudley said, as instructed by the teenaged king who had been the one to feed him the newest allegation earlier that day.
This one, of course, being true.
John Dudley, nor anyone among the council, knew of their king's sudden wish for the death of his own uncle and cousin, but the anger which reverberated off of him of late – much like his late father's – suggested it was not a matter to be questioned. Instead, they had swiftly ordered their arrest and were now busying themselves in finding reasonable claims to attach to them for a hasty execution.

"It is conspiracy, then," the king said, replying to Dudley's remark, "Planned treason to interfere with and overthrow the king's government."
The members of the Privy Council looked at one another, Dudley and Cecil nodding at the men beside them.

"That might be cause enough for an execution," Cecil summarised, though there was no enthusiasm in his tone.

"Good," King Edward said briskly, "See to it that it is done!"

January 1551

Edward Seymour did have a trial.
But it was of no use, the king's desire to remove any trace of him and his family being great enough to allow for false statements to be made against him.
And so, at the beginning of the new year, the king's only surviving uncle was sent to the scaffold, to be beheaded for treason.
"Dearly beloved masters and friends," Edward Seymour said as he sniffled audibly, "I am brought hither to suffer, although I have never offended against the king neither by word nor by deed. I and my family have always been faithful and true unto this realm and His Majesty. But as I am by law condemned to die, I –"
His final speech was suddenly interrupted by the arrival of two horsemen.
The crowd before the scaffold at Tower Hill turned wide-eyed to observe the men on horseback, then back to the red-faced Edward Seymour before them.
"A pardon!" some began to shout, before almost all of them echoed, "A pardon! God save the king!"
But it was not a pardon, the men on horseback merely coming to make sure the crowd remained peaceful throughout the beheading.
The brief light which had ignited in the condemned man's eyes flickered out as he realised that he was to die after all, and he finished his speech, this time even more tearful as before.
"I have always been most diligent about His Majesty in doing his business," Seymour muttered as he knelt down before the

block, "and no less diligent about the common service of the whole realm."

He let his face be covered with his handkerchief then, before laying his head down on the wooden block.

And just before the axe cut through his neck, he managed to pray, "Lord Jesus, save me."

August 1551

With the near-scandal behind him, King Edward was once again able to sleep at night, knowing that his secret was safe.

At the age of almost fourteen-years-old, it was becoming increasingly difficult to suppress his sexual urges for his best friend. Especially when Barnaby had grown up to be the athletic and handsome young man that he was.

It was *almost* as though he were trying to entice the king, so well-built was he.

Edward would often catch himself daydreaming about having been born a pauper instead of Henry VIII's long sought-after Tudor heir. For had he been born anything but the Prince of Wales, with the inherent understanding that he would father his own sons and continue the Tudor line, Edward might have been able to live his life as he would have wanted. It would have been in secret and in the shadows, but it might have been possible.

As King of England, where he was never alone and where it seemed even the walls had eyes and ears, Edward would never be able to slip up. Not even for a moment.

To partake in sodomy was illegal. Edward knew that.

And yet he tried to read between the lines when he brushed up on his father's laws about it.

The Buggery Act passed by Henry VIII in 1533, when he had broken from Rome and the Catholic faith, expressly forbade any sexual activity not related to procreation, regardless of gender involved in the sexual act.

It included anal as well as oral sex, and it had initially been an Act to solely clamp down on Catholic priests who had claimed to be celibate simply by not fornicating in the way that would conceive children.

Therefore the Buggery Act was, essentially, another clever way of removing Catholic priests and their practices from King Henry's court and country when he had proclaimed himself Supreme Head of the Church of England.

And it was now the one law his son, King Edward, wished his father had never passed when he had turned to Protestantism.

For it was the one law which was disallowing him from exploring his true feelings for his best friend.

Well, he thought, *That, and the fact that Barnaby has explicitly told me that we would never be more than friends.*

Edward sighed at the wretchedness of his situation, and he considered how much easier his life would be if only he were attracted to women.

Lord knows his father had had the greatest of all appetites for them. And yet his only legitimate son had not a morsel of interest in what existed between a woman's legs.

Despite the young king's knowledge that he must never give in to his temptations, he couldn't help but want his love interest to be near him whenever possible.

Which was why Edward created him – as well as John Dudley's fifth son, Robert Dudley – a gentleman of the king's Privy Chamber.

As a gentleman of the Privy Chamber, Barnaby and Robert would wait and attend to the king in private. It would be their position of duty to the crown.

And it meant that Edward would get to see Barnaby every single day.

With this gift to himself, Edward promised that he would accept his fate as the fiancé of the princess of France, and that he would let go of his selfishness in regard to procreation.

When the time came to wed, he would do so. And cheerfully. Seeing as it was his duty to his late father, as well as to the Tudor dynasty and his people.

He would force himself to lay with a woman for as many times as it would be necessary to conceive a male heir.

He would do this willingly. Knowing that he would have Barnaby waiting on him, hand and foot, for the remainder of their lives. And knowing that, when the time came to physically thrust inside a woman, he would simply allow his mind to envision her to be Barnaby.

After all, there was no law that said he could not *imagine* himself fornicating with a man.

Yes, Edward had planned it all out. Marriage did not have to be so bad. He could do this.

He *would* do this.

It was the only way Edward would be able to do his duty, while also trying to stay true to who he was.

October 1551

Over a year after the Treaty of Boulogne had been signed, the French king Henry II sent his governor, Maréchal St. André, to visit the English court to negotiate the marriage between the young King Edward and the even younger Princess Elisabeth of Valois.

The princess was but six-years-old, Edward reminded himself with a smile as he greeted the French governor to his court.

Giving him six whole years of freedom before the princess was of age to marry, and another two years after that before they would be expected to consummate.

This would be a perfect match for him, after all.

"Governor!" King Edward called from his gold throne beneath the large and beautiful stained-glass window in the great hall.

"Your Majesty," the Frenchman replied with a bow.

"I heartily invite you to dine with me at tonight's banquet," Edward drawled, flashing his straight, white teeth, "we may talk details after dinner. And tomorrow we shall hunt with the hounds."

During the course of the festivities over the next couple of days, a marriage settlement was agreed upon after some haggling over the princess' dowry.

And following the French governor's departure, Edward sent his six-year-old bride a fine diamond – one reserved from the collection of the Queen of England's jewels – to signify his commitment to waiting for his bride to mature.

As he knew would be expected of any soon-to-be husband, Edward stood for a portrait the following week, to send as a gift to his future bride.

He chose to have a life-sized panel portrait created – mirroring that of his father's – to show off his stature.

France sent one of the Princess Elisabeth in return two weeks later – although this one was no more than a bust portrait – along with a letter from the little princess herself claiming that she stood before Edward's painting in her chambers every day to bid him good-day.

Despite Edward's aversion to the female form, he couldn't help but smile at the letter. Whatever the princess may grow up to be, in this precise moment Edward could admit that the little girl was certainly sweet. And if her dedication to being a good wife were to continue into adulthood, Edward was sure she would do nicely as the mother to the future kings of England.

And yet, while he secretly celebrated his precisely devised plan, it would never come to pass.

For Edward never would marry, or even meet, his little fiancé Elisabeth of Valois.

Chapter 14

November 1551
Greenwich Palace, London

"It is important your court learns about European politics and warfare, Your Majesty," archbishop Cranmer was telling Edward as the teenaged king sulked over the latest news.
His council had selected several of the king's household to travel to France for the foreseeable future.
And Barnaby had been one of those chosen few.
"As the Treaty of Boulogne has joined our two countries," Cranmer continued, "We must take advantage of their European knowledge."
Edward knew he had to nod, though his body felt stiff with heartache.
The thought of not seeing Barnaby every day felt like a punch to the gut. And although his best friend had never, and likely would never, reciprocate his feelings, Edward liked to know that his friendship was constant and true.
Barnaby had never told a soul about the king's secret. And Edward knew he never would. He would stake his own life on Barnaby's loyalty.
And though he had also never expressed his opinions on it, Edward knew Barnaby did not think less of him for it.
To him, he was just Edward. His friend.
He was the only one who truly knew who Edward was.
And now he was to be taken away from him.
"How long?" the king managed to ask.
Cranmer shrugged, engrossed in the backgammon game between them, "No more than a few years."

Edward's face drained of colour but he continued to stare, silently at the table, knowing that to protest too much would be a guaranteed way of getting people to start talking.
Instead, he swallowed the bile that had risen in his throat and nodded his head, before moving his piece of the board in victory. Cranmer shook his head in dramatic defeat.
Edward knew Cranmer had allowed him the victory, as ever. But for the first time, it didn't feel so great.
This time, it made Edward think how much he would miss Barnaby's company. For he was the only one to ever truly treat Edward like he was just any other person.

December 1551

Edward wrote his friend almost every day during his first month in France, reminding him to focus on the task ahead – to further his education of the European ways.
But Barnaby being Barnaby, he would reply with letter upon letter gushing over the French women.
Their red lips.
Their sultry glances.
Their foreign dances.
Even of their outlandish abilities under the sheets.
Or behind a bush in the middle of the day, if it took their fancy.
Barnaby was truly in his element in France, Edward thought.
And he could not even begrudge his friend. For he knew that if given the chance, he too would be fornicating at every given opportunity.
But that did not mean Edward did not feel a sting of jealousy towards those wanton women and their effect on his friend.
And, as any scholarly king ought to do, Edward replied in the same way to each of Barnaby's letters.

My dearest friend,
Do not be so easily swayed by the opposite sex and resolve in finding fulfilment in learning and reading of the Scripture.
I ask you to, as far as you may, avoid the fairer sex's company. Yet, if the French king command you, you may sometimes dance with them.

Edward knew Barnaby would take no notice of his king's order, for only he knew that it came from a place of jealousy rather than kingly command.
But Edward felt better in wording his request, knowing that he had done what he could to remind Barnaby what he meant to Edward while they continued parted.
In the hope that one day upon his return, his friend would see Edward as more than just his ill-fated chum.

April 1552

Though King Edward had always been a healthy child – other than his battle with quartan fever some ten years prior – he was suddenly struck down with measles *and* smallpox.
"The king will die," John Dudley duke of Northumberland said in a rash whisper as he, William Cecil and Archbishop Cranmer hurried through the dimly lit hallways of the castle.
Cecil shook his head, "He is strong," he countered, "He may yet survive!"
Dudley exhaled abruptly through his nose as they took a sharp corner and entered the courtyard. They hurried through it, the shine of the moonlight guiding their way towards another dark hallway.
"We must make arrangements in case the worst should happen," Dudley said.

"Surely not, sir!" Cecil replied, shaken by Dudley's remark, "We ought to send word to his sisters, no doubt. But despite that, there should be no cause for betraying the king on his sickbed."

"We must pray he recovers," Cranmer interjected quietly, like a snake slithering between two wolves, "If he *were* to die…his Catholic sister would succeed him."

Dudley raised his eyebrows at Cecil as though to say, *See?*

But Cecil continued aghast, "He will pull through," he said, his green eyes shining with determination.

The young Secretary of State stormed off then, shaking his head at his two colleagues for uttering such disturbing conclusions.

"He is hopeful," Dudley said as he and Cranmer watched Cecil leave, his dark hair bouncing with determination to get away from the treasonous conversation.

Cranmer scoffed as he too stared after Cecil, "He is naïve."

Ten days had gone by since the teenaged king had been taken ill.

Ten days in which his physicians had forced awful-tasting boiled barley water down him to temper his fever.

Thankfully, after three days of lethargic consciousness, the barley water had indeed aided the king out of his feverishness.

But this had been when the spots had spread from the inside of his mouth to his face and down his chest.

They had itched uncontrollably and ached, a dull throbbing beneath the skin where hard, pearl-shaped bumps had appeared. It had kept the king up at night, writhing uncomfortably as the agony of it all had overcome him, so much so that his physicians had concocted another barley mixture, this time with poppy and wild lettuce, to help the king sleep.

But it had been the sulphur-based ointments that had hurt more than any other symptom or ailment, the crusty and scabbed up spots burning horribly upon application, which the doctors had believed to be essential for the king's recovery.

And, thanks to the king's very best physicians, King Edward had emerged seemingly recuperated.

William Cecil had looked upon his fellow councilmembers with a smug expression, their frantic fretting having been needless, for their strong king had fought off not one but *two* deadly diseases all at once.

Sadly, what not even the king's best physicians had known, was that while the king had outwardly recovered, his body continued drained and suppressed from the attack of the two illnesses. And that, were he to catch even the slightest of chills in the following months to come, King Edward VI would most certainly not be so lucky again.

And, had Cecil been aware of this, he may well have joined his colleagues in their scheming to supplant the king's Catholic heir, his sister Mary.

The Book of Common Prayer had been deemed a political failure.

While its goal had been to lead England into one single Protestant fold, and to finally deviate from any and all Catholic beliefs, it had succeeded only in antagonizing Catholics, as well as many Protestants.

"They are saying it is not clear enough, and too similar to traditional Roman Catholic services," Dudley informed the Privy Council, but addressing Cranmer directly, since it had been he who had largely written it, "and that it does not address the central issue of mass – whether it is a miraculous sacrament or a commemorative service."

Cranmer scoffed and opened his mouth to speak, but King Edward cut him off.

"Re-write it, archbishop," Edward ordered, his eyes flickering with disappointment.

"The first publication caused uproar, Your Majesty," Cranmer replied, dumbfounded by the king's decision, "This will lead to more outcry!"

"I'm sure," Edward replied, "But it will lead to *Catholic* outcry! And cease the Protestant! I cannot have both religions displeased with the Book of Common Prayer. We must amend it and satisfy those who support the king's faith. Let the Catholics continue offended, as long as Protestants are in agreement that the king's book is law, that is all I care about at this point. Those who endure in their upheaval are aiding nought but placing a target on their own backs, for it will make it that much easier to single them out and have them burned as heretics for their Catholic beliefs!"

November 1552

Some months later, the Book of Common Prayer was revised to be explicitly reformed in its theology, removing all doubt as to whether *some* Catholic doctrines were allowed.
For they were not.
This second edition of the Book of Common Prayer made it clear to all of England that to simply *be* a Catholic, in whatever minor scale, was illegal and cause for execution.
The newly revised prayer book had now removed any and all remaining traditional sacraments that the previous version had kept, including anything that reflected belief in the blessing and exorcism of people and objects. It also removed prayers for the dead, since this implied the existence of Purgatory, which was a Catholic belief.
These ceremonies were henceforth altered to emphasise the importance of faith, rather than trusting in rituals or objects.

For the months that followed, commissioners were appointed to inspect all the churches throughout the country for compliance with the new reforms.

Churches were aggressively stripped of everything but the bare essentials for worship, the commissioners seizing candlesticks, altar cloths, chalices, and any decorative item deemed unfit for Protestant worship.

And it sent the king's Catholic sister Mary into a tailspin.

January 1553

"I do not feel well, my lords," fifteen-year-old Edward mumbled as he held his head in his hands, interrupting John Dudley's ramblings about the country's newest uproar, this time regarding inflation.

Dudley looked down at the king, then at his fellow advisors, with wide eyes.

"Your Majesty?" Cecil muttered, reaching across the table to place a hand on the king's shoulder.

Edward moaned, his eyes closed.

"He is hot to the touch," Cecil said as he pulled his hand away.

The chaos that followed was immediate.

"Call the physicians!"

"Hurry, help the king up."

"You, boy, come help us with the king."

With the help of the king's servants, Edward was able to stumble to his bedchamber. Once inside he was stripped and laid to rest in his great royal bed, the king's physicians buzzing around him frantically to determine the cause of his latest fever. But it was only once the night had swallowed the sun and the castle had grown dark and cold that Edward began to show signs of what might be wrong.

The cough that developed as if out of nowhere was dry and persistent. And the more it continued, the more raw Edward's throat became.

"What is the cause of this, doctors?" archbishop Cranmer asked the king's best physicians later that night.

The bearded men all looked at one another, not one of them able to answer the archbishop.

"If the fever persists throughout the following days…" one of them said, leaving the archbishop in shock with the open-ended remark.

Cranmer turned from the physicians and strode hastily down the corridors to inform his fellow advisors, shaking his head in anger at the young king's inability to simply remain healthy.

"Not again…"

King Edward's fever did not break for several days, his cough having continued hoarse and dry. But now, Edward would often hack up green sputum, which his servants were ordered to wipe away with a cloth, since the king was too weak to do it himself. Over the next few days, his legs had begun to swell and though his fever had thankfully broken, the phlegm the king continued to bring up had developed into a pinkish, and sometimes black, colour.

"The matter he ejects is like the colour of blood," the king's physician told John Dudley on the morning of the seventh day, "His Majesty has also developed ulcers across his body, which continues swollen still."

Dudley rubbed his hand over his temples, irked rather than worried, "Is there improvement, at least? Do you know what the cause of it is?"

The physician averted his gaze in shame, wordlessly giving the Duke of Northumberland his answer.

Dudley waved the bearded old doctor away, annoyed by his cluelessness. Then he exhaled sharply and headed to the council chamber, where the rest of the Privy Council were waiting.

All the men raised their heads towards Dudley as he entered, their eyebrows high on their foreheads in question as to the young king's health.

Dudley only shook his head in response and the councilmembers' shoulders sagged.

"We must make plans," Dudley said as he stood at the head of the council table beside the king's empty gold throne.

Cranmer nodded, "As per the late king Henry's will, the Lady Mary is King Edward's successor. We *cannot* let that happen..."

The men around the table nodded.

Even Cecil agreed, "While I support the late king's will in all things," he said carefully, "I am in favour of avoiding the Catholic Lady's coronation."

"All our work towards the reformation would be undone," Dudley summarised.

"The Lady Elizabeth it shall be then," Cecil said, logic demanding that if they planned to skip over the next heir for her Catholic faith, then the heir to follow being of the Protestant faith would make her the perfect candidate.

But Cecil noticed Cranmer, Grey and Dudley sharing a look.

"My lords?" Cecil asked, narrowing his eyes.

"Henry VIII bastardised both his daughters," Cranmer explained, "And we are claiming to surpass the Lady Mary due to her illegitimacy – not her religion. If we support instead her Protestant sister, who too was made illegitimate, our cause would be discredited."

"But it is her right..." Cecil said, flabbergasted by his councillors' lack of loyalty.

"Come off your high horse, Cecil!" Dudley said angrily then, "You are just as much working against the Lady Mary as we are. Do not spout out about rights and laws. We are *all* in agreement that the king's Catholic sister must not rule. And for us to have a leg to stand on we cannot support her equally illegitimate sister."

Cecil lowered his gaze and remained silent, for though he did not like to admit it, Dudley was right.

And Cecil was being a hypocrite.

The men looked around at one another then as a silence had ensued, suggesting the matter concluded.

"Do we include the king in this?" Henry Grey asked, to which Cranmer raised an eyebrow.

"It would be wiser to do so," Cranmer said, "In case the king does recover."

Dudley nodded once, "It is decided then," he said, "Now all we must do is convince the king to go against his lord father's wishes."

Cranmer stood from his seat, "Leave it to me, my lords."

Despite Edward's rapidly deteriorating condition, his mind remained sharp – albeit fatigued – and it didn't take much to convince him that it would be in the country's best interest to prevent the accession of his Catholic eldest sister.

"I love Mary the most," he mumbled after he had agreed to his advisor's plan, "But I am my father's son. And I must –" he stopped to cough violently then, his face turning purple with the effort to bring up the black mucus.

A servant appeared from the shadows and wiped Edward's mouth, then offered him a sip of small ale before returning to his post.

The king fell back against his cushions and sighed heavily, "I must put my legacy before family. Mary must never sit on my throne. See to it that she does not."

Cranmer nodded but remained silent, eager to exit the chambers before he had to witness another of the king's disgusting coughing fits.

March 1553

Over the following weeks, the king's council devised a plan that would see the late king Henry's line of succession revised to entirely surpass his two bastardised daughters by his first and second wives, and to instate his fourth named heir as King Edward's successor instead.

This heir was the Lady Jane Grey.

Though her father, Henry Grey, had previously worked in cahoots with Thomas Seymour in the hope of betrothing his daughter to the young king, Henry Grey now thanked the Good Lord that his plan had not taken form. For if their union *had* gone ahead, his daughter would not have been Queen of England long if the young king were indeed to perish from this illness, as his physicians seemed to believe he would.

Things were set in motion for Jane to take the throne of England in her own right, the sixteen-year-old Protestant daughter of Henry Grey being completely unaware of this plot as it took shape.

"She cannot rule uncontrolled," John Dudley said one night as he, Henry Grey, Cranmer, and Cecil sat around a wooden table in the great hall.

It was late, so late that they were the only remaining courtiers awake, the fireplace having nothing but glowing embers within it at that hour.

"Who do you suggest?" Cranmer asked, though he had some idea as to who Dudley had in mind for a husband to the next queen, since the duke had five sons to offer up.

Dudley shrugged as though he hadn't considered it, "my son Guildford is of similar age to the Lady Grey. And he is a comely, virtuous and goodly gentleman."

"Isn't Guildford to marry Margaret of Clifford?" Cranmer asked, a smile playing on his lips, "King Henry's final option listed as his successor in his will, behind Jane and many others?"

Dudley shrugged, "Betrothals can be revoked," he said.

Henry Grey, too tired and too dim to comprehend the unspoken reason for Dudley's change of mind for his son's wife, simply shrugged.

"So, it is decided?" Cecil asked, his brows furrowed, uncomfortable with the entire situation.

"Decided!" Dudley announced, "Jane Grey is to marry Guildford Dudley. And together they shall be the next king and Queen of England."

Cecil exhaled and stood from his seat, desperate to remove himself from such treasonous announcements, "*If* King Edward dies," he added to Dudley's inappropriately gleeful statement.

May 1553
Durham House, London

Jane Grey, as great-granddaughter to Henry VII, and grandniece to Henry VIII, had therefore a direct claim to the throne of England through her legitimate bloodline.

But above even all that, Jane Grey was an excellent candidate for the king's council as England's new monarch, because Jane was very openly and staunchly a Protestant.

She had had an excellent humanist education thanks to her royal lineage, and a reputation for being exceptionally learned for a young woman.

And today, Jane Grey would be made to marry a young man she had never met, in order to fulfil her father's long-awaited wish that his daughter would be of some use to him on his quest for power.

"Why ought I be made to marry one of the duke of Northumberland's youngest sons?" Jane Grey asked, more attentive than most young women, "He offers no lands or standing to the marriage, as a man ought to when marrying a lady of high birth."

"You may be my first born and most valuable daughter," Henry Grey replied, "But that will not spare you from a whipping if you do not do as I command."

His threat was not empty, Jane knew as much from many years of physical abuse at the hands of her dim-witted father, who saw a threat in anyone with more mental capacity than he…which was most people.

Jane raised her chin, "I shall do your bidding father," she replied, "As I know it is my duty to obey. Though I do stand by my confusion for this hasty and sudden match."

Henry Grey scoffed, "Your confusion may persist," he said uncaringly, "It is not your concern to know everything."

Jane curtsied quickly at her father's snide remark and left the room to ponder the new information.

Guildford Dudley was not a man of worthy status, as she would have expected in a husband, since she was the eldest granddaughter of the late king Henry's favourite sister, Mary Tudor. As an heir to the throne of England, surely a more noble man would make more sense for her husb –

Jane's mind stopped short as a thought occurred to her about her chosen betrothed.

He was indeed the sixth son of a duke – the duke of Northumberland – and therefore came with little to no titles or land to his name. Yet he *was* the son of the duke of Northumberland nonetheless. The same duke who was Regent in all but name to the young King Edward…

Could his council really be planning to –

No, surely not.

The king's heir was the Catholic Lady Mary. And her sister Elizabeth after her. Jane was not to attain the throne unless the king *and* his two sisters were to die childless. That was what was in king Henry VIII's final will and testament.

Could her father really be devising a plan to *usurp* not one but *two* of the king's heirs, in favour of his own daughter on the throne?

Her?

Jane frowned, her stomach clenching with dread as she considered this ludicrous plan.

It would surely never work, Jane knew this, the people's love for the Lady Mary being far greater than King Edward's Protestant council wished to admit.

She sighed deeply and pressed on towards her chambers, shaking her head.

Jane would have to trust that her lord father would not risk his family on a reckless pursuit of the throne of England, for no doubt even *he* would know that it would only end in bloodshed…

The young lady realised she could do nothing but hope her father would not stoop so low. But upon second thought, Jane knew it would not be enough to hope. And she concluded instead to pray to God.

For only He would be powerful enough to save her soul from ruin if her father's plan were indeed as she feared.

July 1553

Edward was surrounded by his Privy Council, archbishop Cranmer and John Dudley standing on either side of his great royal bed, their expressions of disgust and disappointment no longer hidden from him.

His complexion was an unearthly grey, his eyes surrounded by dark purple shadows, and his head looking too big for his fragile body.

The sick king had been half-propped up by his many feather cushions in an attempt to raise him, so that he could sign the newly devised document that declared Jane Grey his heir.

"Is it…done?" the young King Edward whispered hoarsely as he handed the quill back to his advisor.

Dudley nodded once in response to the king, fighting his urge to grin with delight; for his son and new daughter-in-law would rule England before long. Just as soon as King Edward were to die, which – according to all the physicians – would be any day now.

He could no longer keep down any food and was wracked with constant pain throughout his swollen body.

His cough persisted, black sputum often speckling his chin and bedsheets without warning before a servant would rush to his side and wipe his mouth.

And still the physicians continued in the dark as to what their young and formerly healthy king was dying of.

One by one, his advisors began to exit the king's chambers, Dudley and Cranmer at the lead without so much as a quick bow of their heads.

Edward was of no more use to them.

Henry Grey and William Cecil lingered for a moment, though Grey was quick to follow the other two like a lost puppy.

Only Cecil remained, his eyes shining with emotion for the young king. But then he too departed, his chest aching with sadness.

Edward was left to rest alone, with his few servants in the shadows, which was how it had been for most of the past six months.

Edward considered his lonesome surroundings once his advisors had closed the door behind them, and he was troubled to realise the mirroring reality of his equally lonesome childhood.

Much like in the last six months, Edward had never truly been alone, constantly surrounded by servants, yet he had felt utterly isolated despite their relentless presence.

He had learned to accept it years ago, knowing that his lord father was busy on his quest for a spare son as well as the beginning of the country's reformation. Not to mention the politics and the wars…

It was all too much for Edward to even consider now, while his head felt heavy, and his eyes throbbed behind their closed lids.

"I am glad to die," Edward said aloud to no one in particular, knowing no one of worth was even listening.

He briefly considered how his life might have continued had he not become stricken with this mysterious ailment. How he would have married the French Princess Elisabeth upon her twelfth birthday and perhaps fathered a son by her.

That is, if he would have managed to push aside his disgust to do his duty.

He had had the inclination to do so to continue the Tudor line. He would have done it all: the wedding, the consummation, the pretending to be something he was not.

He had been prepared for all of it.

And yet, he would have lived a lie.

Edward was seized by a coughing fit again then; his body almost too weak to even spit out the offending mucus.

A servant boy sprang forward as if out of nowhere and held a handkerchief to the king's face as Edward coughed violently, his face beaming red with effort.

When the phlegm was ejected and wiped away, Edward fell back against his cushion and inhaled deeply before opening his eyes slightly.

Through the delirium and exhaustion, he looked up at the servant boy standing over him and saw suddenly the friendly face of his best friend Barnaby.

Though he had not actually returned from France.

"Barn –" he mumbled, raising his hand slightly off the bed.

The servant boy heard the king's muttering and remained at his side for a moment, unsure of what he ought to do.

"You came back," Edward whispered, his heavy eyes opening and closing slowly with fatigue.

The servant laid the dirty handkerchief on the king's bedside table. Then he slowly sat down on the king's four-poster-bed, aware that the poor young king was no doubt believing him to be someone else.

Edward reached over and took the servant's hand gently.

"I am faint," Edward muttered, his head lolling to the side as he tried to look into Barnaby's sea-foam green eyes.

Just one last time.

"I am here, Your Majesty," the servant boy replied carefully, squeezing his king's hand in companionship.

"Oh Lord God," Edward mumbled, to which the servant boy hung his head and closed his eyes to listen to the king's prayer, "save thy chosen people of England! My Lord God, defend this realm from papistry and maintain thy true religion."

A shiver ran down Edward's back then, "I am faint," he mumbled again, before looking up into the servant's eyes and seeing not his dark brown gaze staring back at him, but the green eyes of the young man Edward had loved in secret.

The servant leaned forward then and tentatively wrapped his arms around the king, fully aware that it was against protocol to do so, but caring little for it, knowing that the poor young boy was otherwise to die utterly abandoned.

Edward's heart soared to be held by his love. The only person who had ever truly known all of him, and he allowed himself to melt into Barnaby's embrace.

He finally felt at peace.

"Lord have mercy on me," Edward whispered against the servant boy's shoulder as memories of Barnaby flashed before his mind's eye.

His lopsided grin as he beat Edward at chess.

The naughty twinkle in his seafoam-green eyes when Edward had pushed him into the hedgerows.

His mischievous laugh when he spoke of girls.

Edward inhaled deeply one last time then, hoping to take some of Barnaby with him into the afterlife.

Even if only a trace of him.

"Lord have mercy on me, and take my spirit..."

Epilogue:

Just as Jane Grey had predicted, her marriage to John Dudley's son, Guildford, had been no more than an elaborate ploy for her father and John Dudley to rule England through her.

"I do not want it!" Jane said, her voice shaky yet firm in tone.

"It is done," Henry Grey, her father, replied, "The late king's Act of Succession is signed by him, and it is clear. He declares you his heir, surpassing his sisters due to their illegitimacy."

Jane shook her head, taking a step back only to bump into her new father-in-law. She swivelled round, her eyes wide and shining with fear.

"The people will not stand for this," Jane said as she looked from one power hungry man to another, "You underestimate the people's love for their princess."

Henry Grey shot John Dudley a quick, frightened look then, which Dudley dismissed with a wave of his hand.

"We hold London and the king's army," Dudley replied, "The Lady Mary has no support and no means to fight her way into London."

Jane swallowed hard, her stomach lurching with nausea as she realised it did not matter. Whatever the outcome, she would likely never be safe again for as long as she lived.

And she was suddenly no longer sure which outcome she feared more.

That Dudley might be right, or that he would be wrong.

End of Book 3

Author's note:

I urge the reader to remember that my work is fictional.
The creative liberties I do take, however, never impact the bigger picture or the final outcome, as I believe that history should not be distorted so greatly that it's unrecognisable.
With that being said, I'd like to share with you that Edward's close friendship with Barnaby is true. Edward's letter to Barnaby in France, urging him to stay away from women, is also true. Whether he was homosexual, however, is of course no more than a theory.
Edward's manipulation from a very early age is true. Cranmer, Edward and Thomas Seymour, Dudley…they all scrambled to control the young king for their own political gains and needs.
In my humble opinion, Edward – though born a boy, and favoured – suffered greatly for being Henry VIII's child. Though his suffering was arguably less harrowing than Mary's and Elizabeth's, he too was given the challenging task of mending the broken kingdom he had inherited, after decades of Henry VIII's tyranny and selfishness had torn it to pieces.

My take on Jane Seymour's death is not as far-fetched as you might believe.
Historians have mixed opinions about her death, new research suggesting that a pulmonary embolism could have been the cause. However, Henry's involvement is fictional.

My depiction of Anne of Cleves brought me great joy, as I personally do not think her to have been as ugly as Henry would like us to believe. Portraits of the time certainly suggest that she was anything but 'ugly', and I always thought there must have been another reason for his distaste. Her inability to know his fragile ego needed checking might very well have been the tiny detail that had caused his reaction.